Everyday Problems and the Child with Learning Difficulties

BEBE BERNSTEIN

JOHN DAY BOOKS IN
S E
SPECIAL EDUCATION

The John Day Company NEW YORK

Published on the same day in Canada by Longmans Canada Limited.

Library of Congress Catalogue Card Number:
67-14606

PRINTED IN THE UNITED STATES OF AMERICA

Acknowledgments

From the time of birth, a child must learn to solve problems in order to survive in his environment. As the child grows, he observes how daily problems are handled at home. Today, as an adult, I look back with greater understanding on the life situations my mother and father faced. In my role as teacher and parent, I continue to marvel at the child's ability to adjust to new situations. The child with special problems has even deeper learning obstacles to overcome. This book was written with an awareness of the educational implications for the child who is different.

There are many who have worked toward diminishing the problems of the special child. This book materialized because their philosophies influenced me. These include the staff of Brooklyn College, where I was introduced to the field of Special Education by Prof. Louis E. Rosenzweig, Irwin Goldstein, Leo Shainman, and by Prof. Chris J. De Prospo of the City College of New York.

Through my husband, Owen Bernstein, and his active participation in the related field of rehabilitation, I was always a part of the pioneer efforts of those who made indents into unexplored areas. As Supervisor of the Mentally Retarded, Division of Vocational Rehabilitation, and through his activities in such groups as the Governor's Committee on Mental Retardation, he made many contributions toward solving the problems of the special child as an adult. Men whose work became meaningful to me through the years include Dr. Salvatore Di Michael, of the Department of Health, Education and Welfare. Dr. Max Dubrow, Jerome Nitzberg and Jack Tobias were part of a group who laid the foundation for workshop experience for the mentally retarded.

There are agencies and organizations that have pioneered work in Special Education. In New York City, we are fortunate to have facilities that have contributed to this growth. The Bureau for Children with Retarded Mental Development, administered by Director Katherine D. Lynch, guides teachers who presently work in more than 900 classes. As part of this complex, I have had the opportunity to relate to such different groups as the Bureau for the Education of the Physically Handicapped; Bureau for Speech Improvement, Early Childhood Division; Bureau of Child Guidance, and those concerned with the brain-injured, emotionally disturbed and socially disadvantaged.

In concert with educators, parents have affected the course of Special Education. Parents, exemplified by Joseph Weingold, have become leaders who have brought the needs of the mentally retarded to the public. They have demonstrated how people can handle deep life problems with courage and action. I know, because their problems have touched me.

The difficulties involved in the mechanics of assembling this book were solved enthusiastically by Robert Ross, and daughters Freya and Karen. The typing dilemma was approached with patience and efficiency by Romaine Horowitz and Sylvia Hochberg. As always, my husband Owen's suggestions attenuated the numerous crises that develop in the growth of a book.

To all my problem solvers, thank you.

BEBE BERNSTEIN

Contents

Problems

Situation Problems

Concept Problems

Applied Information Problems

1. Introduction to Problems in the Environment

Daily living experiences may become problem situations for the mentally, socially or emotionally deprived child. If the child is a slow learner, mentally retarded, or if he has had limited environmental opportunity for experience, a simple encounter may become a problem.

The problem may have its inception in the home, school or greater community. In this book, life problems are delineated and a method is presented for solving each one. The approach is to teach the child by developing awareness, utilizing familiar experiences, providing an environmental vocabulary, concrete learning aids and the means of solving problems.

The teacher who has worked with children with learning difficulties understands the need for this type of realistic approach. No problem is considered too elementary. Problems whose solutions appear obvious to us can interfere with the child's routine daily life and his ability to function fully in the community. With each problem, the teacher should consider the following questions:

1. What is the nature of the problem?
2. Why is it a problem for the child?
3. When or where does the child encounter the problem?
4. How can the problem be solved?
5. What learning aids can alleviate the problem?
6. What are some other related problems?
7. How may the problem solution be transferred to other areas of learning?

In the process of considering these questions, it is hoped that the teacher will develop a way of thinking that brings greater understanding of the deprived child's problem needs.

The book also provides the teacher with a means of surveying the experiential background of a class. This will help in understanding the culturally disadvantaged child, the slow learner, or the retarded child, each of whom requires a direct approach to the problems he encounters. The book aims to fill the gap between the demands of the environment and the child's ability to handle problems of daily life.

II. Objectives and Goals

The child with learning difficulties, more than others, needs guidance in coping with life problems.

Children are eager to learn about the world around them. An important educational objective is to stimulate and satisfy this curiosity and interest. The child needs help in orienting himself to his physical environment, since as an adult he will live in this same natural world. How can we prepare the child for the problems he will experience? The concepts taught should be those that will actually be used in life situations.

Experiences should contribute to social and emotional development. Familiarity with problem situations minimizes fears and frustrations and provides security. A positive approach is therefore stressed throughout the book.

Social experiences, however, often present themselves as problems. Daily living problems become a threat to the mentally retarded or slow learner because of his limited capacities. An important objective, therefore, is the development of a method that stresses positive and concrete thinking.

Problems of health and safety arise in the child's life. Science concepts can be utilized in these areas to teach safety or good health practices and attitudes. Science and safety problems that are significant for the child with limitations center on emergency situations, traveling in the community, or using machines that are part of his daily living. Science for this child is developing awareness of his environment and learning how to cope with it. The mentally handicapped child does not need to know, for example, the scientific principles involved in the construction of a vacuum cleaner. For him, it is more meaningful to know how the machine works and how he can use it. It is important that he learn how to use an elevator and what to do if it breaks down while he is in it.

Preparation for adult life includes preparation as a citizen, a social being, and a worker in the community. If we teach the child the importance of repairing tools, we are preparing him for adult responsibilities.

By making the child aware of situations in which he can easily be led astray, we are preparing him for adulthood. Mentally handicapped children are easily influenced and have difficulty in using good judgment. For example, the child should be aware of the dangers involved in accepting gifts from strangers or opening the door indiscriminately. He should be made aware that when he orders items from a store, he is responsible for payment. (Can he read the form? Is the item free? Is there a cost?)

A significant life goal is preparation for the world of work. An early beginning is necessary to prepare for economic goals. To build respect for the kinds of jobs the slow learner will do, appropriate work areas should be explored early. Slow learners and mentally retarded adults may be employed as truck helpers, delivery boys, restaurant and hospital workers. It is important, therefore, that the child learn how to use a wagon to load groceries, how to stack supplies so that they do not fall, and why foods should be refrigerated. He can learn these concepts by actually stacking objects and by observing what happens to milk if it is not refrigerated.

It is the teacher's responsibility to become aware of the implications of daily living problems and to be alert to the techniques that will enable the child with learning difficulties to solve them.

SUMMARY OF TEACHER OBJECTIVES

1. Stimulate the child's curiosity and interest in his environment.
2. Utilize scientific principles and concepts that the child can understand and that will help him in a problem-solving situation.
3. Provide experiences to teach the child how to cope with this physical world.
4. Prepare the child for his adult life as a worker, citizen and social being.

5. Help the child to function independently in his home and in the greater community.
6. Assist him to develop positive attitudes toward safety practices.
7. Guide him to develop sound health habits.
8. Encourage pupil participation and verbal expression.
9. Develop an environmental vocabulary that will help the child function in his surroundings.
10. Provide concrete learning aids and experiences that will help him solve problem situations.
11. Develop an awareness of each child's special needs in the solving of everyday problems.

III. Application of Everyday Problems

Problem solving demands a form of reasoning that may sometimes be too abstract for the child with learning difficulties. His limitations, which may be due to a mental disability, social handicap or emotional disturbance, are reflected in the manner in which he handles problems.

To be appropriate, therefore, a problem should be one that the child has met or will meet in his life activities. If it is a situation that interferes with his ability to function independently, then it is appropriate for consideration.

Although the child is unable to think abstractly, this should not exclude him from participating actively in solving problems. Problem solving can be accomplished through experimentation, observation, demonstrations or discussion. Note, for example, Problem 5 – Why do you paint things? Soaking two pieces of wood, one painted and one unpainted, in water is an experiment that demands observation to see what is happening. The children discuss why paint helps protect their houses. They learn that it is their responsibility to keep their homes in good condition. They also learn that paint accomplishes this. (How?) These concepts are taught by approaching the problem directly and solving it by utilizing concrete experiences that involve the children.

Learning takes place also through associations (Example: fire can burn!). Developing associations demands a more highly developed form of thought process. If the associations are familiar, concrete and tangible, they can be utilized to provide solutions for problem situations. See, for example, Problem 20 – Which door would you use? This problem involves the selection of the proper door to use when entering a store or building. The concrete associations or learning aids are the signs IN and OUT. By observing and reading the signs, the child learns what to do. In the process, a verbal and reading vocabulary is developed. This environmental vocabulary provides further associations (Examples: HOT, ELEVATOR, BARBER SHOP, STOP, etc.). Other associative learning aids may include colors, objects, people, shapes, or words, for example, Problem 18 – Which handle would you PULL? This situation involves the task of mailing a letter. How does the child know which box is the correct one, the mailbox or the fire alarm box? What are the learning aids and environmental vocabulary words involved in teaching the child to recognize each?

Signs: MAILBOX, FIRE ALARM BOX
Colors: Red and blue, red
Words: U.S. MAIL, In case of fire . . .
People: The child learns that the mailman uses the mailbox, he works in the Post Office; the fireman protects us, he lives in a firehouse.

Curiosity is an important factor in stimulating thinking, a factor which teachers can utilize to motivate the child. Sometimes, focusing upon a situation arouses curiosity that may lead to negative actions or behavior (Example: topic – false fire alarms). Since the child, especially the slow learner or mentally retarded, can be easily influenced and may often act without adequate judgment, a concrete thinking approach is indicated. Positive rather than negative attitudes should be developed.

The skillful teacher also uses questions and discussion to encourage the child to express himself. Problems are thus shared by pupil and teacher. The following excerpt from a guided discussion demonstrates this technique. The group consisted of primary level, educable, mentally retarded children.

A. Problem: Why should you brush your teeth?

B. Materials: crackers, toothbrush, toothpaste

C. Method

1. Experiment I
   a. The teacher chose two children (Billy and Steven) to eat the crackers.

b. Billy and Steven chewed and ate the crackers as the class watched.
c. We then examined their mouths.

2. Observations
 a. What do you see?
  Paul: "Dirty mouths."
  Linda: "Teeth has crackers."
  Richard: "Billy ate all of his cracker."
  Peter: "No more cookie!"
 b. Where are the crackers?
  Susan: "Crackers stay in the teeth."
  Mary: "You get holes from dirty teeth. I brush my teeth every day."
  Robert: "Some crackers stay in the teeth. Some go into Steven's stomach."
 c. How can you get the crackers out of Billy and Steven's mouths?
  Responses: "Take a drink of water." "Brush our teeth." "Pull out all the teeth!"
3. Experiment II
 a. Steven drank water and we noted that the crackers still remained in the "cracks" of the teeth.
 b. Billy brushed his teeth and we noted that the teeth and "cracks" were clean.

D. Conclusion: We brush our teeth after eating to keep them clean.

In applying a problem-solving approach to a situation, the handicapped child's questioning and reasoning power should be utilized within his limitations.

IV. Organization and Approach to Problems

Different kinds of environmental problems arise in the process of everyday living. The ones explored in this book are categorized as Situation Problems, Concept Problems and Applied Information Problems.

A. Situation Problems

1. The situation problem centers on the child's life in the home and away from the home.
   a. Problems of self-sufficiency
      Example: Which toilet would you use? (No. 24)
   b. Problems involving care of the home, machines, tools and appliances
      Example: Which tool would you use? (No. 6)
   c. Problems that the child encounters in the street and neighborhood environment
      Example: Which handle would you PULL? (Mailbox or fire alarm box?) (No. 18)
   d. Problems of the child as a social being and a member of a greater community
      Example: What do you do at the MOVIES? (No. 25)
   e. Problems that involve preparation for adult life, work and the development of responsibilities
      Example: Why do you paint things? (No. 5)
2. Each problem situation is considered through utilizing the following format:
   a. Statement of the problem is presented in the form of a question.

b. Materials necessary for use with the problem are listed.
c. Method of solving the problem is presented, with alternative solutions.
d. Solutions to the problem are reached and stated.
e. Learning aids and environmental vocabulary related to the situation are listed.
f. Related problems for further consideration are suggested.
g. A problem worksheet with teacher directions accompanies each situation problem. The worksheets illustrate pupil assignments that may be completed with direction from the teacher. They can be the culmination of a lesson or they can provide oral and written review of what has been learned. The worksheet examples included in the book present various methods of applying what was developed in the lessons. The worksheets demonstrate the range of exercises that may be planned, using pictures or words. The worksheets are included as a guide for the teacher, to help in developing similar material appropriate for the group or individual child.
h. Suggested activities and follow-up assignments culminating from the lesson are related to other curriculum areas.

B. Concept Problems

1. The concept problems are designed to enhance the extent of the child's awareness and absorption of environmental stimuli.
   a. How familiar is he with his surroundings?
      Example: How many ways can you travel? (No. 28)
   b. How can he improve his adjustment to his surroundings?
      Example: How do you learn what is happening to people and places? (No. 29)
2. The concept problem aims to expand the child's knowledge of such concepts as color, shape, symbols and direction.
   a. Example: What do the COLORS mean? (No. 26) Traffic lights – how do colors help to keep us safe? What is the color of the policeman's uniform? What color indicates DANGER?
   b. Example: What do the arrows tell you to do? (No. 30) Where have you seen them? What do they mean?
3. Each concept problem is structured as follows:
   a. Purpose and aims are stated.

b. A worksheet with teacher directions is included with each problem. The teacher may use the worksheets for group assignments or with the individual child. The exercises may be utilized orally or in written form. They help to reveal the child's conceptual strengths and weaknesses.

C. Applied Information Problems

1. Applied information problems aim to:
   a. Familiarize the child with himself and help him to apply this information to a problem-solving situation.
   Example: What should you know about yourself in an EMERGENCY? (No. 34)
   b. Make the child aware of the use of information in relation to objects in his environment.
   Example: Directions on mailbox or fire alarm box. Do you know what the words tell you to do? (No. 35)
   c. Acquaint the child with information in order to minimize problems related to places in the community. Example: How do you use the LIBRARY? (No. 38)
   d. Enable the child to utilize information related to his cultural, social and other daily activities. Examples: Completing simple forms and coupons, using guides and following directions. How do you send for things? (No. 36) How do you find your favorite (TV) program? (No. 37)
2. The applied problems are structured as follows:
   a. The purpose is stated.
   b. Information worksheets with teacher directions are provided. The teacher may work orally or use written exercises with an individual child or group. The information problems provide the teacher with a means of evaluating and understanding the child's difficulties.
   c. Additional activities are suggested. The teacher should be encouraged to construct questionnaires and develop other applied information problems related to the specific cultural needs of the individual child or a particular social or ethnic group. (Note: Other topics are suggested in Chapter IX. Example: What would you do if . . . ?)

V. Methodology

In order to utilize fully the suggested techniques, materials and activities, the teacher should become familiar with the methods outlined below.

A. Teacher Preparation

1. Prepare for each lesson by becoming familiar with the procedures and by noting the appropriate problem worksheet.
2. Prepare materials before introducing the lesson (materials section).
   a. Use the suggested materials list that accompanies each problem.
   b. Prepare suggested word flash cards related to the learning aids and environmental vocabulary listed with each problem (learning aids and environmental vocabulary section).
   c. Prepare drills or homework assignments related to the problem. Consult sections on drills, reviews, and additional activities.
   d. Check to determine whether children have working materials (pencils, worksheets, crayons, etc.).
3. Become familiar with the method of arriving at the solution of problem.
   a. Review the method section that accompanies each problem.
   b. Note that solutions are reached by discussion, demonstrations, experiments, etc.
   c. Review the solution section that accompanies each problem.

4. Teacher Directions
   a. The sections on teacher directions explain how to use the accompanying problem worksheets and how to help the child complete his individual worksheet.
   b. Teachers should become familiar with these directions before developing the lesson.
   c. Use the worksheets as indicated in the directions. They may be part of the lesson development or used as related exercises at the conclusion of the lesson.
   d. Review directions with the group. Teacher or child reads directions aloud. Be certain that all children understand what is required. Discuss each direction carefully.
   e. Exercises and assignments should consider different ability levels within the group. For example, some children draw a picture, others write the word (see Chapter IV).

B. Lesson Development

1. Motivation: Motivate each lesson. The following means of motivation are suggested in the introductory material that accompanies each lesson (method section).
   a. Children's experiences
   b. Picture discussions
   c. Presentation of a situation
   d. Stories, poems, riddles
   e. Questions
2. Techniques
   a. Experiments
   b. Demonstrations
   c. Exploratory situations
   d. Observation
   e. Group participation
   f. Recording of information
3. Questions
   a. Use questions suggested with each problem as a guide. Questions should stimulate thinking and active participation in reaching solutions.
   b. Present questions simply.
   c. Make questions concrete.
   d. Reword questions to guide children toward a problem solution. Provide additional information if child does not give correct response.

e. State questions appropriate to the group's level of understanding.
f. Questions may be utilized to discover what the child has absorbed about his environment.
g. Encourage children's questions.

4. Vocabulary
   a. Introduce new words related to the problem. Words are listed with each problem.
   b. Utilize word flash cards.
   c. Use blackboard for clarification, games, drills and review.
   d. See following section, "Meaningful Vocabulary."
5. Summaries
   a. Review what has been learned at different points in the lesson.
   b. Use medial summaries.
   c. Use final summaries.
   d. Review concepts, words and solutions.
6. Worksheet Exercises
   a. Discuss directions orally.
   b. Assist children in completing each exercise.
   c. Check each child's work carefully.
7. Follow-up Procedures
   a. Provide drill and review.
   b. Check vocabulary concepts related to the problem.
   c. Provide homework assignments.
   d. Provide additional activities in related curriculum areas (mathematics, language arts, social studies).
8. Other Considerations
   a. Consider one problem a week initially. Be flexible according to group's mental level and interest.
   b. With experience and exposure, the child will respond increasingly to the problem-solving approach. Increase the time allotted accordingly. Note that an individual problem may have several lessons inherent in it.
   c. Consider different mental capacities of the group in reading and written work related to the problem. Note different assignments for different levels.
   d. During the week, provide vocabulary drill and review opportunities. (See sections on charts, additional activities, and techniques.)

e. Wherever feasible, relate the problem to the current class topic. For example, Community Helpers, Food, Stores, Safety in the Street, etc. Note and use sections on related problems.

f. Be prepared for unexpected responses. Example: In the problem that involves an errand to a store (Which door would you use?), the story notes that the store is closed. According to the story, the child returns to his home. One pupil suggested that the child find another store. Teacher: "A very good idea! However, in the story Peter went home." Encourage these individual responses.

C. Meaningful Vocabulary: Developing the Environmental Vocabulary

1. Reading Goals
   a. Acquaint the child with a variety of reading experiences which he may encounter in his environment.
   b. Provide motivational reading materials for a problem situation.
   c. Teach the child to recognize and read signs that stress safety and protection.
   d. Provide reading exercises that aim to evaluate concepts and learning.
   e. Summarize facts through stories and charts.
   f. Teach the child to handle his environment by stressing functional reading.
2. Reading Materials
   a. The worksheets include examples of stories or charts appropriate for the child who is reading on a primary level.
   b. Either the teacher or a child may present the reading materials according to directions.
   c. Experience charts, stories, experiments, and other worksheet reading resources may be prepared and used by the teacher as the basis for a regular reading lesson.
   d. Identify all pictures. Use labels whenever feasible.
   e. Read and clarify all captions that accompany pictures.
   f. Consider different ability levels in the written exercises.

3. Teach the environmental vocabulary words according to methods used for introducing any new word.
   a. Use pictures or stories.

b. Review meaning of the word.
c. Note configuration and spelling.
d. Consider the sound. Say the word.
e. Use other techniques (Example: kinaesthetic).

4. Note that environmental vocabulary words are usually written in capital letters. The child sees them in this construction in his daily life (BOOKS, TELEPHONE, STORE, PUSH, PULL, etc.).
a. Capital letters are used in the book when appropriate to the problem.
b. When the child writes the environmental vocabulary word, encourage him to use capital letters.

5. Reinforce learning through:
a. Drills
b. Reviews — oral and written
c. Charts
d. Games
e. Experience charts, stories, and books
f. Visual materials (pictures and films)
g. Exercises — oral and written

6. Encourage children to keep lists of environmental vocabulary words.
a. Children may construct their own sets of word cards and keep them in boxes to use for individual study or games with other children.
b. Children may keep notebooks in which they list the vocabulary words.

D. Concrete Learning Aids

1. Learning aids should be stressed by the teacher during the development of the lesson.
a. See sections on learning aids.
b. See sections on teacher directions.

2. Provide additional review through the following:
a. Charts (Examples: colors, shapes)
b. Books related to topics (Example: the fireman)
c. Pictures related to topics (Example: toilet articles)
d. Signs and labels (Examples: door, OPEN, traffic signs, etc.)
e. Problem worksheets and other written exercises

3. Become familiar with learning aids listed with each lesson.
   a. Signs
   b. Labels
   c. Names
   d. Objects

E. Additional Activities

1. Classroom activities are suggested with each problem. These activities are listed after each section of teacher directions.

2. Types
   a. Activities related to other curriculum areas
   b. Trips, visits and special events
   c. Activities that meet the needs of varying ability levels and groups within the class
   d. Exercises to be utilized as independent activities
   e. Activities involving visual materials
   f. Experiences centering on related problems and topics

3. Independent activities: exercises appropriate for children who are able to handle more formal activities. Examples:
   a. Use a word in a sentence. Draw a line between picture and word, two words, etc.
   b. Use the word in a story (vocabulary).
   c. Find these words in the story.
   d. Alphabetize words.
   e. Write word meanings.
   f. Construct a word dictionary.
   g. Read books and cards related to science, health and safety concepts.
   h. Develop experience charts or stories utilizing environmental vocabulary.

4. Exercises appropriate for children who need less formal activities
   a. Drawing pictures to depict environmental vocabulary or learning aids
   b. Cutting and pasting activities
   c. Games – match cards, match words and pictures, "pick-a-card" (for two children), etc.
   d. Dictated stories related to topic
   e. Copying signs

f. Copying labels
g. Books related to science, health and safety
h. Which picture is correct? What's wrong with the picture?

F. Visual Aids

1. Pictures – commercial, children's work
2. Books – science, health, safety series
3. Charts – pocket, experience, directions, etc.
4. Films and film strips
5. Objects – traffic signs, etc.
6. Bulletin boards – children's contributions
7. Activity center or area
   a. Display current experiment, keep folders of children's work, shelves for children's worksheets, flash and word cards, children's notebooks, etc.
   b. Keep projects timely. Encourage children to handle materials or demonstration displays. Example: How do you stack boxes and cans? (No. 8)
8. Pocket chart
   a. Use words related to current problem.
   b. Provide additional worksheets for review and drill purposes.
   c. Encourage children to use contents when they have completed other class work and wish additional activities.
   d. Remember – it is the teacher's responsibility to keep the material current.
   Example:

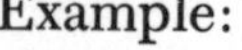

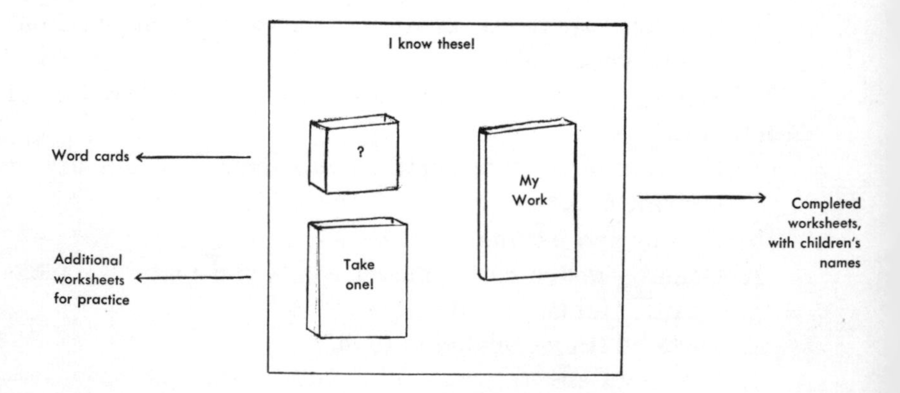

9. Displays related to learning aids
   Example:

A COMMUNITY HELPER

1. Who is he? NAME.
2. What does he do?
3. What tools does he use?
4. What color is his uniform?
5. What signs or words tell you about him?

The policeman, garbage man, painter, postman, etc.

10. Experience charts that summarize demonstrations and experiments (Example: How do you use a nail file? No. 7)
11. Charts related to machines or objects in the community
   a. Use stories and charts on worksheets.
   b. Example: TELEPHONE

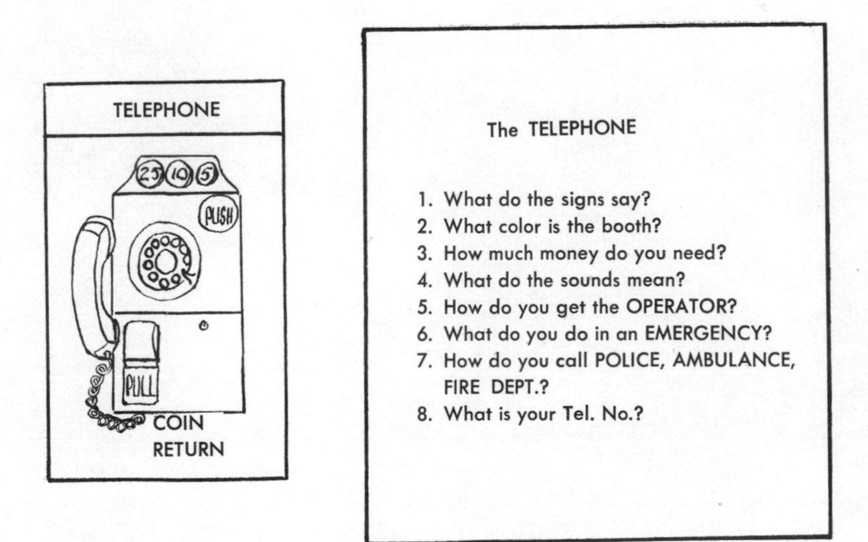

12. Safety signs

a. Make a pocket, containing words. Children match similar words to chart. Use for recognition, review and written work. Copy words. Children play games using chart. Example: Two children – one holds cards. How many can you guess, find, match, read?
Example:

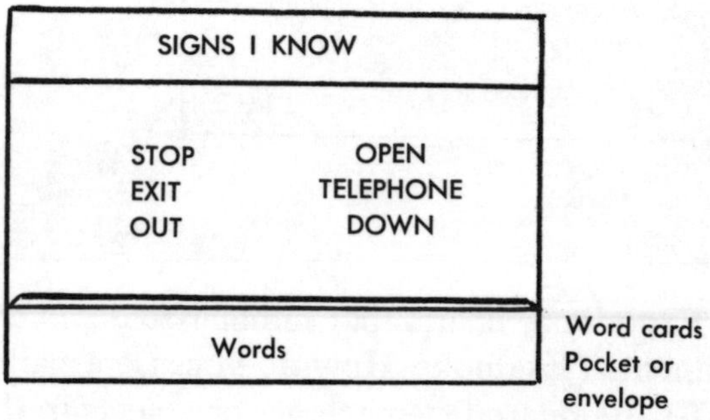

SIGNS I KNOW

STOP
EXIT
OUT

OPEN
TELEPHONE
DOWN

Words

Word cards
Pocket or
envelope

VI. Situation Problems

A. Problem 1

How do you open a can or jar?

B. Materials

A variety of food containers – jars with covers, cans, boxes (cereal, spaghetti), bottles, etc. Can openers (different types). Word cards – PUSH, PULL, OPEN HERE, PRESS, TURN.

C. Method

1. Place the different types of containers on a table before the class.
2. Discuss each container.
   a. Name
   b. What do you find in it?
   c. How do you open each container?
3. Game: Invite children to demonstrate how the different containers can be opened. Teacher's purpose is to discover extent of children's familiarity with the method of opening each one.
   a. Stress safety.
   b. Look at the (can, jar, etc.). . . . Are there words or signs that tell you how to open it?
   c. Tools are sometimes needed to open a box, bottle, can or jar. What would you use? What is it called? How does it work?
4. Containers

a. Jars – TWIST or TURN. Note arrows ↷ What do you do if it "gets stuck"?
b. Boxes – cereal, spaghetti, rice, etc. Some have spouts or covers – OPEN AT THIS END, LIFT HERE or PUSH HERE.
c. Bags – candy, bread, etc. Plastic bags that PULL UP ↑ or PULL DOWN ↓ or have a plastic cord.
d. Bottles – soda or ketchup. Use can opener. Which part?
e. Paper containers – use school MILK containers. PRESS HERE, LIFT UP.
f. Cans – food, soda. Discuss can opener. Which kind? Discuss new pull-up type of can.

5. Review each concept. Stress those that are unfamiliar to the children.

D. Solution

1. Hands and fingers can do many different jobs (TWIST, TURN, PULL, PUSH).
2. Tools perform different services.
3. We should learn to read and follow written directions.
4. By reading signs or words on jars and boxes, we can open them safely.

E. Learning Aids and Environmental Vocabulary

1. TWIST – TURN
2. PUSH – PULL
3. PRESS – LIFT
4. OPEN – CLOSE
5. Arrows UP ↑ DOWN ↓ TURN ↷

F. Related Problems

1. How do you handle glass jars or other breakable containers safely?
2. How do you use other types of household tools?
3. How would you stack or store different food containers?
4. How does an electric can opener work?
5. What other types of packaging are used?

G. Teacher Directions

Problem Worksheet No. 1

1. Review words introduced in other problems:
   PUSH, PULL, OPEN HERE, TURN, etc.
2. Poem on problem worksheet
   a. Read aloud.
   b. Use can, box and jar.
   c. Discuss each picture and sign.
   d. What am I doing? Dramatize each picture (PRESS, PUSH, TWIST).
   e. Demonstration review.
3. In the spaces provided at the bottom of the page, the group may:
   a. Write all the signs they can find in the poem or on containers.
   b. Illustrate the poem or directions.
   c. Write the "Should I" sentence in which each sign (PRESS DOWN, PUSH UP, TWIST THE CAP) is found.
   d. Attempt to write a short poem.

H. Suggested Activities

1. Encourage children to find, write, list, illustrate different types of directions that are found on many types of containers. (Become familiar with signs and words associated with each.)
2. Discuss safety rules related to using various containers: Glass jars, plastic bags.
3. Conduct additional demonstrations in the use of other household tools: eggbeater, openers, knives, peelers, etc. Visit school lunchroom or homemaking room. Provide vocational experiences related to problem.
4. Explain mathematics concepts. Discuss meaning of the numbers found on cans or boxes: 16 ozs., 1 lb., etc.
5. Poetry – listening and writing experiences (see problem worksheet).

No. 1 How do you open a can or jar?

I don't always know what to do,
When I OPEN a can or two.
I don't always know just where,
Should I PRESS DOWN or OPEN HERE?
Boxes are hard when they have a spout,
Should I PUSH UP or PULL OUT?
With jars and bottles I'll never learn,
Should I TWIST THE CAP or make it TURN?

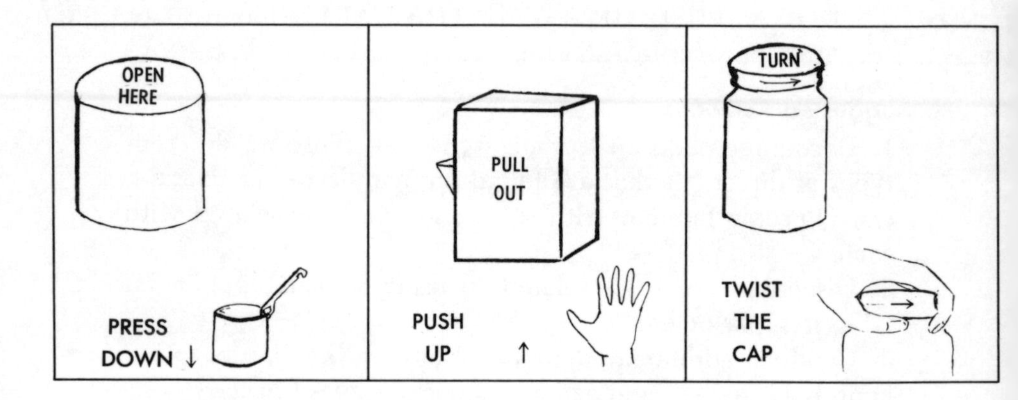

A. Problem 2

<u>Would you use a bowl or plate, spoon or fork?</u>

B. Materials

Variety of food utensils and tools: flat plate and bowl, salt and pepper shakers, sugar bowl and packets of sugar, signs related to topic – RESTAURANT, MENU, SALT, SUGAR, etc.

C. Method

1. Eating at home: tools that help us to eat
   a. Prepare a table setting before the group. (Include fork, spoon, knife, napkin.)
   b. Teacher: Let us pretend (make believe) that we are going to have our lunch. The table is all set. Do you set the table at home? How? You are going to have soup. (Show the children a flat plate and a bowl.) Where should we put the soup? Plate or bowl? Why?
   c. Demonstration A: Pour the liquid (colored water) onto the flat plate. What do you see happening? Pour liquid into bowl. Does the soup stay in the bowl? What kind of food do you put in each plate? What do you put in a cup or glass?
   d. Demonstration B: Invite a child to select the tool he would use to eat the soup. Why? Pretend to use a fork. What happens to the soup? When do you use a fork? What kinds of food . . . ? When do you use a knife?
2. Eating away from home: RESTAURANT
   a. Discussion: Do you ever eat in a RESTAURANT? Do you enjoy . . . ? When? Where? Restaurant manners. Using a menu. The waiter and waitress.
   b. Demonstrations: How do you know which is SALT and which is PEPPER? Read signs. Pour from each. Note the size of holes. Why? Is SUGAR always served in a bowl? (Example: packets)
   c. Examine different types of utensils and containers used in restaurants. How do they work? (Examples: napkin holders, ketchup and syrup jars, etc.)
   d. Review.

D. Solution

1. A variety of tools and implements help us to eat.

2. We use appropriate utensils when we have liquids.
3. We use appropriate utensils when we eat solids.
4. We should learn the names, functions, and proper care of tools used in food preparation and consumption.

E. Learning Aids and Environmental Vocabulary

1. Tools: name and function
   a. Utensils – fork, spoon, knife, etc.
   b. Plate, bowl, cup, glass, etc.
   c. Other tools – strainer, paring knife, etc.
2. Signs related to eating away from home
   a. RESTAURANT
   b. DINER
   c. LUNCHEONETTE
3. Labels
   a. SALT, PEPPER
   b. SUGAR
   c. NAPKINS

F. Related Problems

1. How do you use tools related to food preparation? (Example: mixers)
2. Which direction should pot handles face? (Stove safety.)
3. How do you keep kitchen tools and utensils from rusting?
4. Why should you keep your mouth closed when chewing food?

G. Teacher Directions

Problem Worksheet No. 2

1. Discuss and review concepts developed in lesson.
2. Match them!
   a. Direct children to draw a line from the sign to the appropriate object. Read aloud or use blackboard exercise. (Note: SOUP – spoon and bowl.)
   b. Encourage group to write correct name in space provided under each object.
3. How many do you know?
   a. Survey: Help the children become aware of different signs that designate places to eat away from home.
   b. Questions: Where would you go if you wanted CANDY?

Which place serves breakfast?

4. Writing experiences
   a. Encourage children to add other signs they have seen that designate eating places.
   b. List names (signs) of additional places to eat in the community: COFFEE SHOP, FOOD SHOP, DELICATESSEN, CANDY, SODA, ICE CREAM FOUNTAIN.
   c. List names of workers associated with topic: CASHIER, SALAD MAN, GARBAGE MAN, etc.
   d. List names of different food stores: BUTCHER, FISH MARKET, GROCERY STORE, etc.

H. Suggested Activities

1. Plan a unit of study about the workers who prepare foods and perform clean-up duties (waiter, waitress, dishwasher, garbage collector, etc.).
2. Reading activities
   a. How we read a MENU
   b. Signs that tell us where to eat: RESTAURANT, DINER, COFFEE SHOP, CAFETERIA, etc.
   c. Learn to read recipes.
   d. Follow directions on cans and boxes. (How to prepare canned soup and pudding, etc.)
3. Mathematics: MENU prices and cost; units of measure – tablespoon, cupful, etc.
4. Other demonstrations related to topic
   a. How to use a potholder
   b. How to wash and dry dishes
   c. Using electrical appliances – dishwashers, mixers, etc.

No. 2 Would you use a bowl or plate, spoon or fork?

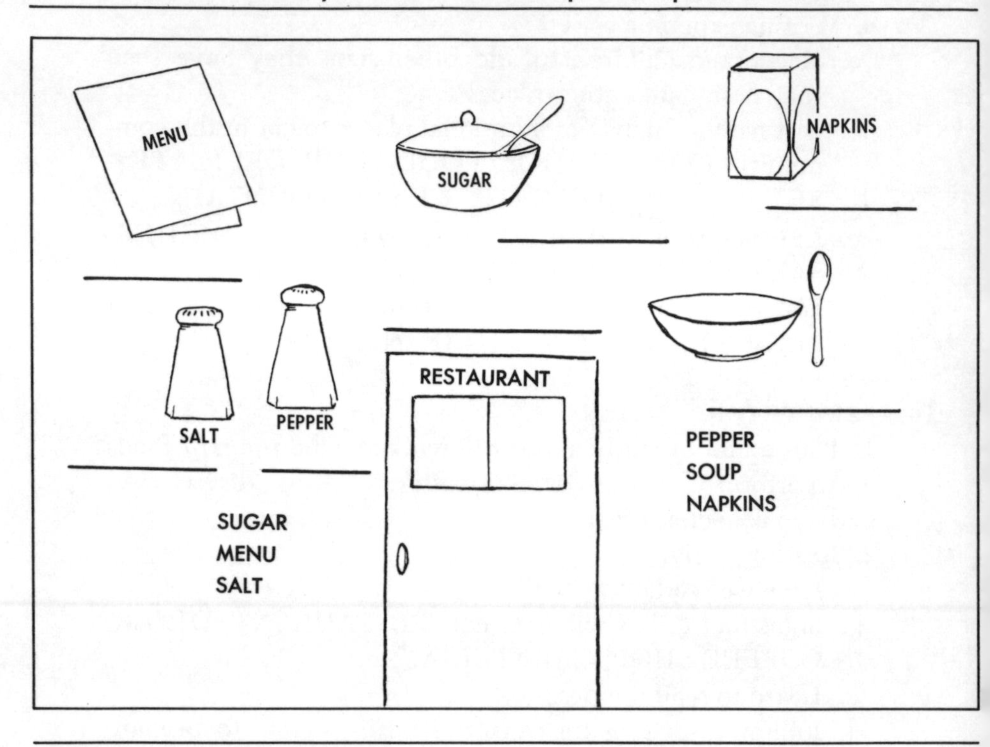

How many do you know?

Places	Things	People
RESTAURANT	CUP	WAITER
DINER	SPOON	DISHWASHER
MEALS	BOWL	WAITRESS
CAFETERIA	FORK	COOK
LUNCHEONETTE	PLATE	BUSBOY

A. **Problem 3**

Why should you keep your house clean?

B. **Materials**

Pictures or objects: BROOM, VACUUM CLEANER, BRUSH, etc.
Labels of different objects used. Refer to method section and worksheet.

C. **Method**

1. Discussion: Do you help to keep your house clean? How? What do you use to dust the furniture? How do you keep your floors clean? Use objects or pictures (Examples: BROOM, VACUUM CLEANER).
2. Review Problem No. 13, Why do you use SOAP?
3. Demonstrations
   a. Use dustcloth. Wipe a piece of furniture or windowsill. What remains on cloth?
   b. Sweep the floor. Use a BROOM or DUSTPAN. Gather the dirt. Repeat this daily. Observe the accumulation of dirt each day.
   c. Examine the accumulation of dirt inside a VACUUM CLEANER, electric broom or carpet sweeper.
   d. Use a variety of brushes to remove dirt. How do you use the brush to get dirt out of cracks? How do we use mops?
4. Related situations: Certain animals and insects make their homes where there is dirt.
   a. How should we protect our clothes from moths? How do clothes brushes help?
   b. How do window screens help us? Observe dust and dirt clinging to screens. Use brushes and vacuum cleaner to clean screens. Keep screens in repair (protection from insects).
   c. What happens when garbage cans are uncovered? (Cats, dogs, mice, etc.)
   d. How do you keep flies away from food?
5. Summarize and review above concepts.
6. Note and record observations – experience chart, experiments, log, etc. Illustrate.
7. Reading experiences – labels associated with problem.

D. Solution

1. Dust and dirt make our homes unhealthy places in which to live.
2. Dust and dirt make our homes unattractive.
3. Certain insects and animals live in dirt and filth.
4. It is our responsibility as citizens to keep our community clean and attractive.

E. Learning Aids and Environmental Vocabulary

1. Concepts: filth, dirt, cleanliness, health
2. Vocabulary: VACUUM CLEANER, INSECTICIDE, DETERGENT, MOTHBALLS
3. Labels
   a. BROOM, DUSTPAN
   b. MOPS, SOAP, WATER
   c. BRUSH

F. Related Problems

1. What other tools or appliances are used to clean the home?
2. Why is it important to keep our houses ventilated?
3. How do window shades help us?
4. Where should you store INSECTICIDES, MOTHBALLS, etc. Why?

G. Teacher Directions

Problem Worksheet No. 3

1. Review names and functions of objects related to problem.
   a. Use pictures.
   b. Use objects.
   c. Match word cards to pictures and objects.
2. "What Am I?"
   a. Read the four signs aloud. Write on blackboard. Match with word cards.
   b. Write label on object. (Provide space.)
3. Riddles
   a. Read each aloud.
   b. Can you guess what it is?
   c. Write correct answer.
   d. Encourage children to make up riddles. Dramatize exercise in the form of a game.

e. Riddles can be recorded as a class chart or booklet. Use other objects.

4. Teacher may use riddles as basis for a reading lesson. Introduce environmental vocabulary.

H. Suggested Activities

1. Labels and signs. Encourage children to label objects used in school and at home – BROOM, DUSTPAN, MOP, SOAP, WATER.
2. Safety unit (develop rules)
   a. How to use INSECTICIDES, DETERGENTS and other products
   b. Electricity: dangers involved in using VACUUM CLEANERS (plugs, cord, outlet)
   c. Animal and insect traps
   d. Dangers from insect and animal bites
   e. Keep foods and garbage cans covered and unavailable to animals.
3. Tools and appliances
   a. How to use brooms and brushes (to wash floors, etc.)
   b. How to use and empty a VACUUM CLEANER, use of different attachments
   c. Using fans and air conditioners for ventilation (discuss dangers and protection)
   d. Compare the efficiency of different tools.
   Examples: VACUUM CLEANER and BROOM; electric rug shampooer and brushes.
4. Vocational skills. Observe workers using different tools and appliances. Children should observe as many actual situations as possible. Examples: porters in office buildings, home cleaning workers, window washers. Provide and encourage actual work experiences.

No. 3 Why should you keep your house clean?

What am I?

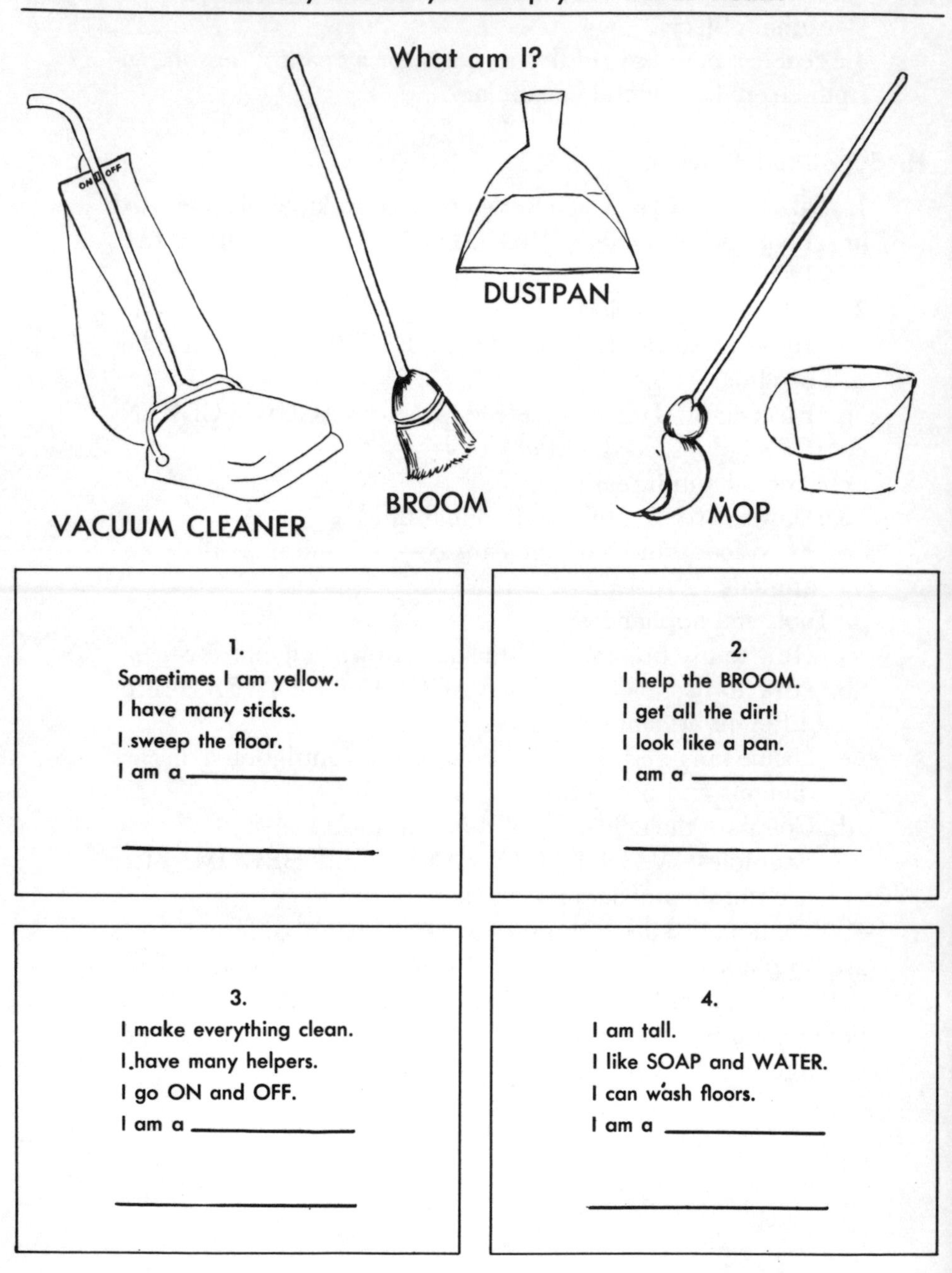

1.
Sometimes I am yellow.
I have many sticks.
I sweep the floor.
I am a ______________

____

2.
I help the BROOM.
I get all the dirt!
I look like a pan.
I am a ______________

____

3.
I make everything clean.
I have many helpers.
I go ON and OFF.
I am a ______________

____

4.
I am tall.
I like SOAP and WATER.
I can wash floors.
I am a ______________

____

A. Problem 4

Why do you put food in a REFRIGERATOR?

B. Materials

Cards: REFRIGERATOR, COLD, ON, OFF
Foods necessary for different experiments (see below)

C. Method

1. Experiments
   a. Compare what happens to meat that is not refrigerated with meat that has been refrigerated. Experiment: Divide a raw hamburger. Refrigerate one piece only.
   b. Compare what happens to foods that are left uncovered with foods that are protected by waxed paper, a plastic covering, or tinfoil. Use bread (moldy, dry), prunes, raisins, etc.
   c. Observe what happens to dairy products that are left unrefrigerated over a period of time (milk, cheese, butter).
2. Record information
   a. Illustrate (using diagrams or pictures) daily observations.
   b. Construct a simple log, chart or book to note observations. (See chart on problem worksheet.)
   c. Plan with children the method for recording information.
   d. Children may dictate their observations to the teacher or write their own stories.
3. Discussion questions
   a. What is happening to the . . . (meat, bread, milk, etc.)?
   b. How does it feel?
   c. How does it look?
   d. How does it smell?
   e. What else is happening?
   f. Why is refrigeration needed? How do "ice and cold" help to keep food fresh? (REFRIGERATOR, COLD, ON, OFF)
   g. How do boxes, cans, bags, plastic, and wax covers protect foods?

D. Solution

1. Food spoils if it is not put in an icebox or a refrigerator.
2. We should keep food covered.

3. Paper, wax, plastic, and tinfoil covers keep foods from becoming dry.
4. Food stays fresh for a longer time if it is refrigerated, covered, or packaged.

E. Learning Aids and Environmental Vocabulary

1. Concept: temperature – HOT and COLD
2. Refrigerator and icebox – names of the appliances that help us
3. Labels: REFRIGERATOR, COLD, ON, OFF
4. Signs: KEEP REFRIGERATOR DOOR CLOSED, KEEP COLD, KEEP REFRIGERATED

F. Related Problems

1. Why should refrigerator doors be kept closed?
2. How do you defrost and clean an icebox or refrigerator?
3. How and why do we use frozen foods?
4. Why is it dangerous to play with old, empty (abandoned) refrigerators?

G. Teacher Directions

Problem Worksheet No. 4

1. Teacher or child reads story aloud.
   a. Review concepts developed during experiments.
   b. Stress labels.
   c. Provide drill of words. Use cards or blackboard. REFRIGERATOR, COLD, ON, OFF.
2. "What do you put in your refrigerator?"
   a. Encourage children to write or draw pictures of foods they would put in the refrigerator pictured.
   b. Provide lists or items from which children may copy labels (milk containers, food labels).
   c. Use newspapers or magazines – pictures and labels.
3. "How does it look, feel, smell, taste?"
   a. Use a simple chart to record progress of an experiment.
   b. Write or draw picture of the food item in the column under FOOD (Example: MILK).
   c. Write or draw a picture in Column 1 of how the food looks, feels, smells or tastes on the first day of observation. Fill in Column 2 – second day, Column 3 – third day (Mon., Tues., Wed.), etc.

H. Suggested Activities

1. Discuss and write up a chart of rules related to the topic. Include use and care of refrigerator, safety and health hazards, other appliances, etc.

2. Trips
   a. Supermarket: Observe how foods are packed – frozen food compartments, dairy and meat departments. Note signs and labels.
   b. House appliance store: Discuss use of different home appliances related to foods (refrigerator, stove, etc.). How do they help us? How should we use them correctly?

3. Other experiments related to foods
   a. What happens to frozen foods when they are not kept in the refrigerator?
   b. Do cooked foods keep better than raw foods?

4. Unit on foods: Discuss different kinds, names, diets, people who handle foods, restaurants, food stores. Teach mathematics concepts – costs of different items, food budgets, SALE, "two for the price of one," etc.

No. 4 Why do you put food in a REFRIGERATOR?

The REFRIGERATOR helps us.
It keeps food fresh and cold.
I keep my REFRIGERATOR ON.
I keep it clean.
I keep the door CLOSED.
I put covers on the food.
I put MILK in the REFRIGERATOR.
What do you put in your REFRIGERATOR?

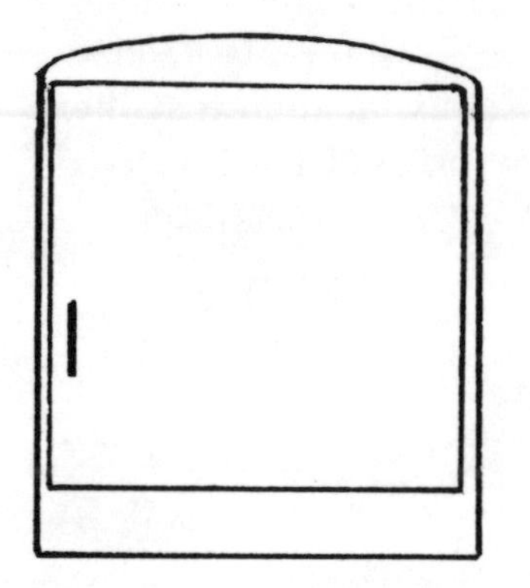

FOOD	How does it . . . ?			
	. . . look?			
	. . . feel?			
	. . . smell?			
	. . . taste?			

A. Problem 5

Why do you paint things?

B. Materials

Two pieces of wood — one painted, one unpainted. Two nails — one painted, one unpainted. Two pans of water. Word cards: PAINT, BRUSH, WET PAINT, PAINTER.

C. Method

1. Discussion: We use many different things to build a house. What are they?
   a. Identify materials (wood, nails, etc.).
   b. Encourage children to name other materials that are used to build a house.
   c. Encourage children to tell about houses that they have observed in the process of being built.
2. Examine materials.
   a. Determine that one piece of wood is painted, the other is unpainted.
   b. Determine that one nail is painted, the other is unpainted.
3. Questions:
   a. Where are wood and nails used to build a house? Parts?
   b. Did you ever paint anything in your house? Shelves?
   c. Are the walls of your apartment painted?
   d. How does paint help? Why do you use paint?
4. Demonstration

   Teacher: We are going to pretend that it has been raining. Rain is water. We are going to put these pieces of wood and nails into the pans of water. Let's see what happens! What do you think will happen to the wood? Nails? Do you think the water will make the paint come off?
   a. Put unpainted nail and unpainted wood in one pan of water.
   b. Put painted nail and painted wood in the other pan of water.
5. Observations
   a. Discuss how each piece of wood looked at the end of the schoolday. And on the next day.
   b. Discuss how each nail looked at the end of the schoolday.

And on the next day.

c. Discuss what you think happens to a house when it is raining. What happens to the nails? What happens when the wood is not painted? Can the rain come in? What is rust?

D. Solution

1. Paint protects the outside of your houses from the elements.
2. Water rolls off painted objects. This should be noted upon examination of painted wood after it has been soaking.
3. Rust can develop on unpainted metals. This should be noted upon examination of the unpainted nail.
4. Paint helps to beautify things.

E. Learning Aids and Environmental Vocabulary

1. Signs related to building a house: MEN AT WORK, KEEP OUT, DANGER, WET PAINT, etc.
2. Concepts: building a house
3. Names of different materials
4. Names of different workers: PAINTER, CARPENTER, PLUMBER, etc.
5. Work associated with building a house

F. Related Problems

1. Should you "hang around" (loiter) near construction areas?
2. How can you help to keep the inside and outside of your home in good condition?
3. What jobs can you do to make your home clean and attractive?
4. What tools can you learn to use?
5. How does rain, snow, or heat affect different materials?

G. Teacher Directions

Problem Worksheet No. 5

1. Read the situation on the problem worksheet "Do You Look?"
   a. Discuss what happened to Peter.
   b. Why did this happen to Peter?
   c. Develop safety rules (WET PAINT).
2. Picture discussion

a. PAINTER
b. PAINT
c. PAINT BRUSH
d. WET PAINT

3. Match the picture with the sentence.
   a. Read each sentence aloud.
   b. Instruct children to write appropriate number.
   c. Encourage child to write or draw a picture of each sign.
   d. Provide drill and additional writing experiences utilizing the environmental vocabulary words.

H. Related Activities

1. Visit or observe a house being constructed.
2. Teach children how to paint an object (Example: book shelf). Stress correct use of brushes, safety, care and cleanup.
3. Visit a hardware store. What materials do you see? Tools? Compile a list.
4. Consider a unit of study related to house, building, or construction workers, to develop an appreciation of manual skills.
5. Provide work experience in related manual skills. Arrange shop work projects.

No. 5 Why do you paint things?

DO YOU LOOK?

Peter went to the park.
He played ball and had fun.
He wanted to sit down and rest.
Peter sat here.
What happened to Peter?

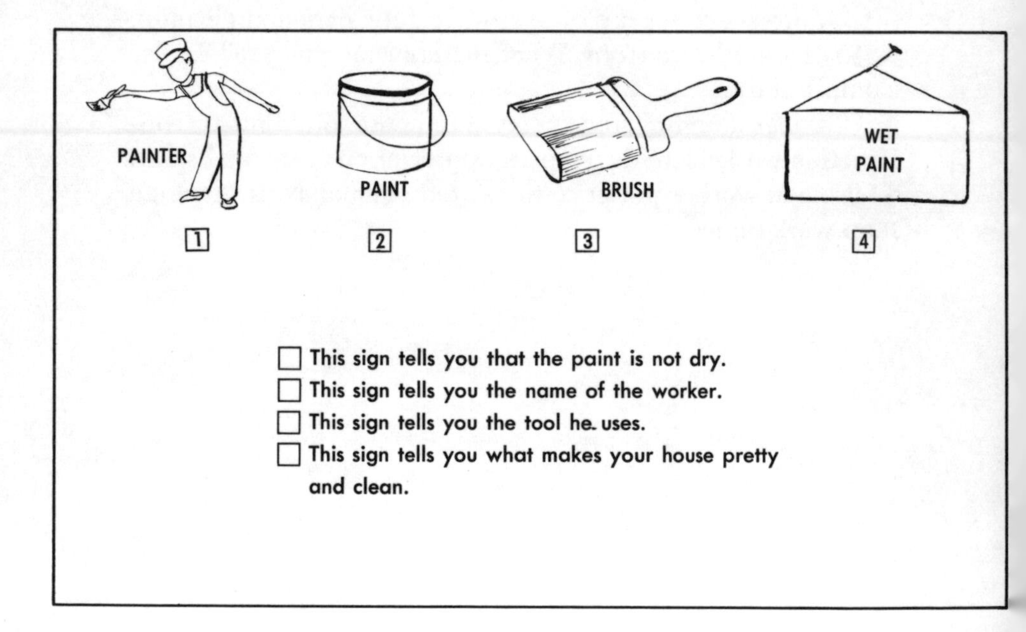

- ☐ This sign tells you that the paint is not dry.
- ☐ This sign tells you the name of the worker.
- ☐ This sign tells you the tool he uses.
- ☐ This sign tells you what makes your house pretty and clean.

A. **Problem 6**

Which tool would you use?

B. **Materials**

Box containing tools or pictures of tools – hammer, saw, pliers, nails, scissors
Two pieces (boards) of wood
Sheet of paper

C. **Method**

1. Situation A: the saw and scissors
   a. Teacher: Father was busy putting shelves together. (What are shelves? Do you see any in our classroom?) He wanted to make them look like this. (Draw a simple rectangular shape with lines.)
   Maybe mother would keep plants on the shelves. Maybe brother would keep books on them. What would you put on the shelves? (Books, toys, games, etc.)
   b. Teacher: Father bought some wood. He knew just how he would cut the pieces. He looked in his toolbox. These are the tools he had. (Use pictures or objects.) He had a pair of scissors and a saw. (Place scissors and saw on table.) What do we call each? Which tool would he use to cut the wood? Why?
   c. Demonstration: Use actual tools. Children cut paper with scissors. Could you use the scissors to cut the wood? Establish that a saw is used to cut wood.
2. Situation B: the hammer and pliers
   a. Teacher: Father was ready to put the pieces together. He looked in his toolbox again. These are the tools he had. (Use pictures or objects.) He had nails, hammer, pliers. (Place tools on table.) What do we call each?
   b. Teacher: He wanted to put the nails into the wood. (Relate to other objects in room that have nails.) Should he use the saw? Which tool should he use? Why?
   c. Demonstration: Use actual tools. Demonstrate that a hammer puts nails into the wood. Pliers pull nails out. Establish the use of each tool. (Could you put nails into wood by using a saw? Pliers? What would happen?)
3. Review

a. Review verbally what was done in Situations A and B.
b. Teacher may record the review in the form of a chart.
c. The review may be recorded by the children in the form of drawings or diagrams.

D. Solution

1. Tools help us in many ways.
2. We use scissors to cut paper or cloth.
3. We use a saw to cut wood.
4. Tools (hammers) put nails into wood. Other tools (pliers) remove nails.

E. Learning Aids and Environmental Vocabulary

1. Names of tools
   a. Scissors
   b. Hammer
   c. Saw
   d. Pliers
2. Oral vocabulary: TOOLS, NAILS, SHELVES, LUMBER, etc.

F. Related Problems

1. What tools help us in the preparation of foods? (Peeler, eggbeater, etc.)
2. What tools do we use in eating? (Fork, spoon, etc.)
3. How should we use tools safely?
4. What tools do different workers use? Who? When? Where?

G. Teacher Directions

Problem Worksheet No. 6

1. Review concepts.
2. "What should you use to . . . ?"
   a. Review name of each tool.
   b. Review function of each tool.
   c. Instruct children to draw a picture or write name of tool needed in each box. (Example: to cut paper – scissors.)
3. Other tools – "Who would use it?"
   a. Discuss name of each tool pictured in column on the left.
   b. Discuss function of each tool pictured in column on the left.
   c. Read the name of each worker.

d. Discuss the job duties of each. Which tool would he use? CARPENTER – hammer; BAKER – mixer; PLUMBER – wrench; BUTCHER – cleaver; DOCTOR – stethoscope; MOTHER – broom; BARBER – scissors, etc.

e. Instruct children to draw a line to match the correct tool with the worker who would use it. Encourage other names: PAINTER, DENTIST, etc.

H. Additional Activities

1. Visit the custodian's workshop, school woodwork shop, hardware store, lumberyard, etc.
2. Observe or invite different workers to demonstrate correct use of tools. Discuss and develop safety rules for use of tools and materials. Learn to write names of workers: CARPENTER, PLUMBER, etc.
3. Label tools and materials in classroom. Encourage children to construct labels and signs – HAMMER, NAILS, SCISSORS, USE CAREFULLY, DANGER, INFLAMMABLE.
4. Develop other demonstrations related to the problem. Experiments may include other tools and materials. For instance, How does mother use a peeler? How do you use a shovel? When should you use a rake, screwdriver, jack, etc.?

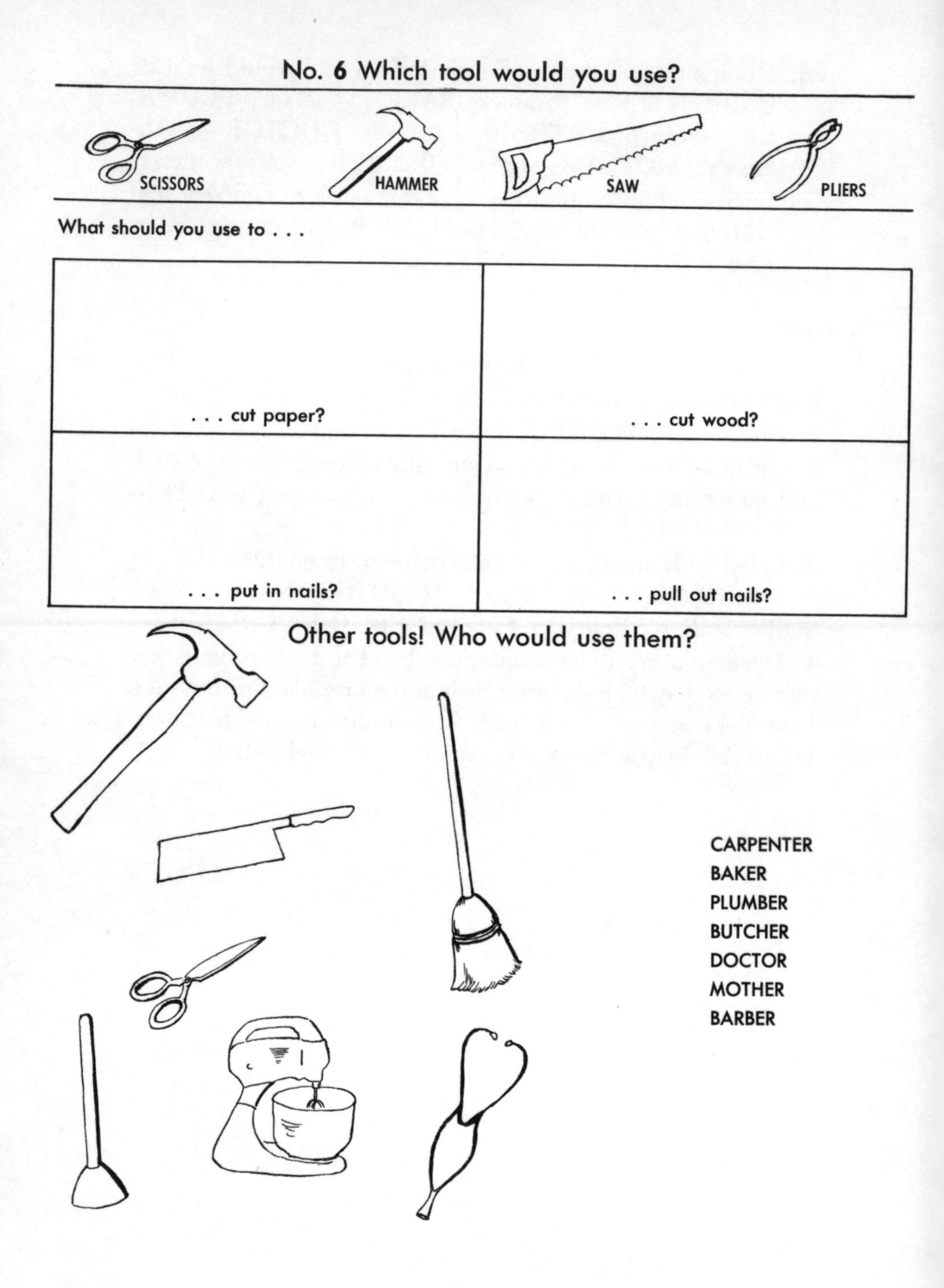
No. 6 Which tool would you use?
SCISSORS
HAMMER
SAW
PLIERS
What should you use to . . .
. . . cut paper?
. . . cut wood?
. . . put in nails?
. . . pull out nails?
Other tools! Who would use them?
CARPENTER
BAKER
PLUMBER
BUTCHER
DOCTOR
MOTHER
BARBER

A. Problem 7

How do you use a nail file?

B. Materials

A variety of toilet articles and accessories — comb, brush, shoe polish, shampoo, hair curlers

C. Method

1. Discussion A: Toilet articles
   a. Familiarize class with toilet articles that help to keep us clean (soap, shampoo).
   b. Use pictures of different articles.
   c. Encourage children to bring in examples of different articles.
   d. Discuss the function of each. (What do they do? How do they help us?)
2. Discussion B: Beauty accessories
   a. Familiarize class with those objects that help to keep us attractive and neat (comb, curlers).
   b. Use pictures of different objects.
   c. Place a variety of objects on a table — bobby pins, iron, hangers, brushes, etc. Discuss their names and function. (How many do you know? What do they do?)
   d. Stress that some objects are toilet articles. Other objects are things that help to keep us neat and attractive. For example, a needle and thread mend our clothes, shampoo cleans the hair and makes it "shiny," irons smooth our clothes and make them appear more attractive.
3. Experiment: Purpose is to set up simple experiments, to encourage observation, and to develop a means of recording information simply.
   a. Nail file
      Compare nails before and after using a nail file. (See problem worksheet story.) Teacher or child brings a nail file to class. Children examine the nail file (point, shape, texture). One child is chosen. Class examines his or her nails. Observe dirt. Use nail file. What happened?
   b. Comb

Have a child comb his hair. Compare. (How does his hair look now?)

c. Iron

Compare ironed and unironed clothes.

d. Shoe polish

Compare two shoes. Use shoe polish on one. Compare polished and unpolished shoes.

D. Solution

1. A variety of toilet articles help to keep us clean.
2. Many different objects help to keep us neat and attractive.
3. We should use toilet articles and beauty accessories daily.
4. Toilet articles (nail files, etc.) should be used carefully.
5. We learn to observe "what is happening."

E. Learning Aids and Environmental Vocabulary

1. Signs
2. Labels: SHAMPOO, COMB, BRUSH, SHOE POLISH, etc.
3. Names of toilet articles and accessories
4. Function of toilet articles and accessories

F. Related Problems

1. Why should each member of a family have his own personal toilet articles?
2. What are the dangers of using nail polish, hair spray, and other similar products?
3. How should you care for your toilet articles (cleaning of combs, brushes, etc.)?
4. Who are the people in the community who help keep us clean and neat (barber, beautician)?

G. Teacher Directions

Problem Worksheet No. 7

1. Review orally.
   a. Develop steps in experiment.
   b. Stress safety factor.
   c. Questions
   d. Summaries
2. Read "We Did This" aloud (problem worksheet).

a. Use story to demonstrate how we can record a simple experiment.
b. Review what was done in other demonstrations (combing, ironing).

3. "What did we do? 1 – 2 – 3 – 4 – 5?"
a. Use pictures to demonstrate that a story or experiment can be told by using pictures.
b. Instruct children to look at the row of pictures. Discuss orally. What happened first? What did we do? Children write numbers according to sequence. Do this exercise with the children. (Answers: 3 – 4 – 2 – 1 – 5)

4. In the space provided at the bottom, encourage children to write or illustrate another experiment that was performed in class.

H. Suggested Activities

1. Experiments and demonstrations. Use pictures or words to summarize other experiments. (See problem worksheet.) Set up procedure.
2. Discuss and set up guide rules regarding appearance (fads, using make-up too soon, extreme hairdos, nail polish, greasy hair, etc.). Limit discussion to problems appropriate to child's level and need.
3. Discuss services appropriate to topic. Barbershop, beauty parlor: money needed, behavior. Become familiar with job duties.
4. Vocational skills: how to iron, use needle and thread to mend clothes, use tie racks and skirt hangers.
5. Mathematics: cost of different articles. Where you buy . . . ? How much should you spend?

No. 7 How do you use a nail file?

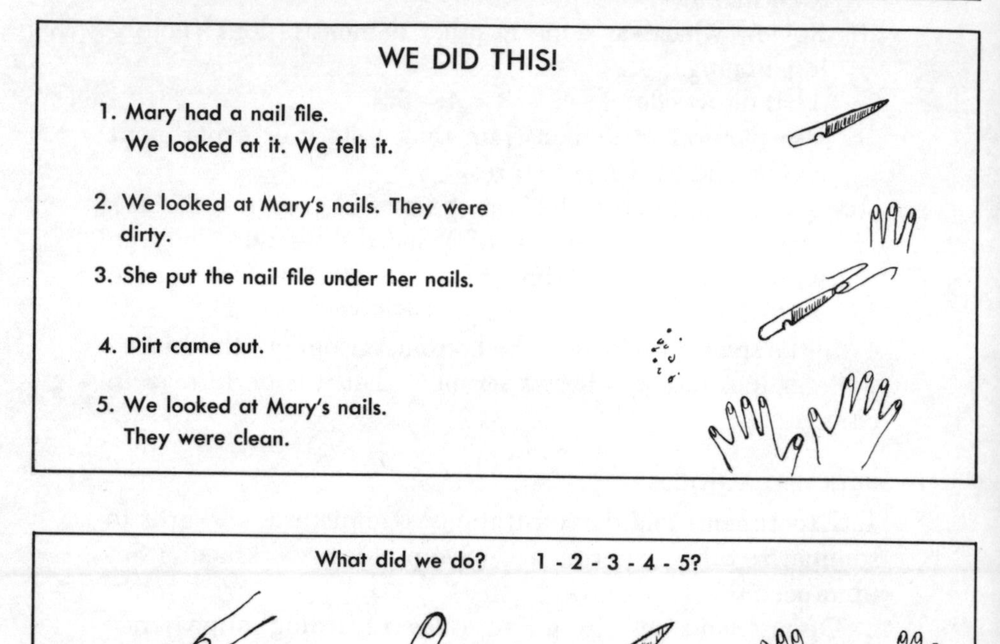

WE DID THIS!

1. Mary had a nail file.
   We looked at it. We felt it.

2. We looked at Mary's nails. They were dirty.

3. She put the nail file under her nails.

4. Dirt came out.

5. We looked at Mary's nails.
   They were clean.

What did we do? 1 - 2 - 3 - 4 - 5?

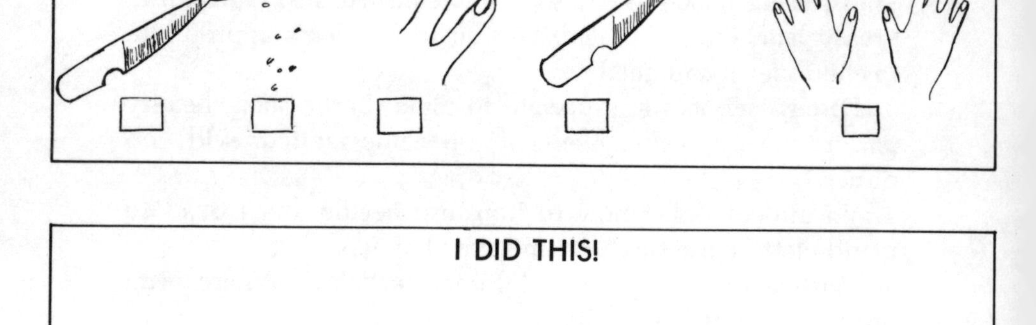

I DID THIS!

A. **Problem 8**

How do you stack boxes and cans?

B. **Materials**

A variety of empty food cans and boxes of different sizes
Blocks of different shapes.

C. **Method**

1. Questions
   a. Do you go shopping?
   b. Do you help put away cans or boxes in the closet?
2. Teacher: Let us pretend that we are going to put these cans and boxes away. Identify each.
3. Demonstration
   a. Teacher places the smallest size box or can on a table (small base).
   b. She places one of the largest boxes or cans on the first object.
   c. She continues stacking (piling) objects of various sizes. She invites class to participate.
4. Observations
   a. What do you see happening? Which one was on the bottom?
   b. Continue the stacking until objects fall or topple. Why?
   c. If the stacked pile does not topple, have a child touch it slightly. Why did it fall so easily? (We had put the smallest one on the bottom.)
5. Pupil participation
   a. Ask children for suggestions. What can we do to keep the cans from falling?
   b. Begin the stacking again. This time place the broadest box or can as the base. (We put the largest one on the bottom.)
6. Repeat using similar sizes and shapes. This experiment may be done using blocks of triangular, tubular or arch shapes. Why didn't they fall?
7. Ask children to stack other objects. Use books, trays, dishes, etc.
8. Review: If you are going to help, which one would you put first, second, third?

D. Solution

1. When we stack cans or boxes, we should place the largest one at the bottom to make a broad base.
2. Similar shapes belong together.
3. It is dangerous to pile objects too high.
4. We stack boxes or cans one at a time!

E. Learning Aids and Environmental Vocabulary

1. Familiar objects have different shapes: boxes, cans, books, dishes, etc.
2. Familiar objects come in many sizes: big and little, long and short, etc.
3. Cans and boxes have labels or pictures that identify the contents.

F. Related Problems

1. What are the danger factors associated with piling and stacking?
2. How do you reach for cans or boxes in a supermarket?
3. What can happen if you carry too many parcels at one time?
4. What can happen if you carry or lift a box that is too heavy?
5. What can you use to move numerous or heavy parcels?

G. Teacher Directions

Problem Worksheet No. 8

1. Discuss and identify pictures on worksheet (a row of cans, boxes, plates).
2. Review concepts.
   a. Rows: How many are there?
   b. Top, middle, bottom
   c. First, second, third
   d. Largest, smallest, middle-sized
3. Do exercises orally at blackboard.
4. Top row
   a. How many cans do you see? Let us count them: 1 – 2 – 3.
   b. Identify largest, smallest, middle-sized.
   c. Teacher: Look at each can. Mother has asked you to put

them in her closet. How would you stack them so that they do not fall?

d. Which can would you put first? On the bottom? Write the number 1 on the can you would put first.

e. Repeat for the second and third cans, writing in 2 or 3.

5. Middle row

a. Follow a similar procedure for the row of boxes or cartons.

b. Child writes the number on each.

6. Bottom row

a. Follow a similar procedure for the row of plates or trays.

b. Child writes the number on each.

7. What's inside?

a. Here are a can and a box. What do you think is inside of each (apples, soap, cereal, etc.)?

b. Have children draw or write (label) the foods or products that could be inside of each.

c. Teacher should prepare children for this exercise by providing magazines or catalogues, and make children aware of labels on containers that are in the room. Encourage similar projects related to labeling.

H. Suggested Activities

1. Encourage monitorial duties in school lunchroom or stock room. Apply learning solution to stacking trays, dishes, books.
2. Food store experiences: Set up store in class, visit a store, write stories, booklets. Read and write labels for cans and boxes.
3. Relate mathematics concepts to topic. Size and shape — big, little, long, short, round, square, etc.
4. Vocational skills: job duties in the home and at work — store helper, stock clerk, etc. Discuss job duties.

No. 8 How do you stack boxes and cans?

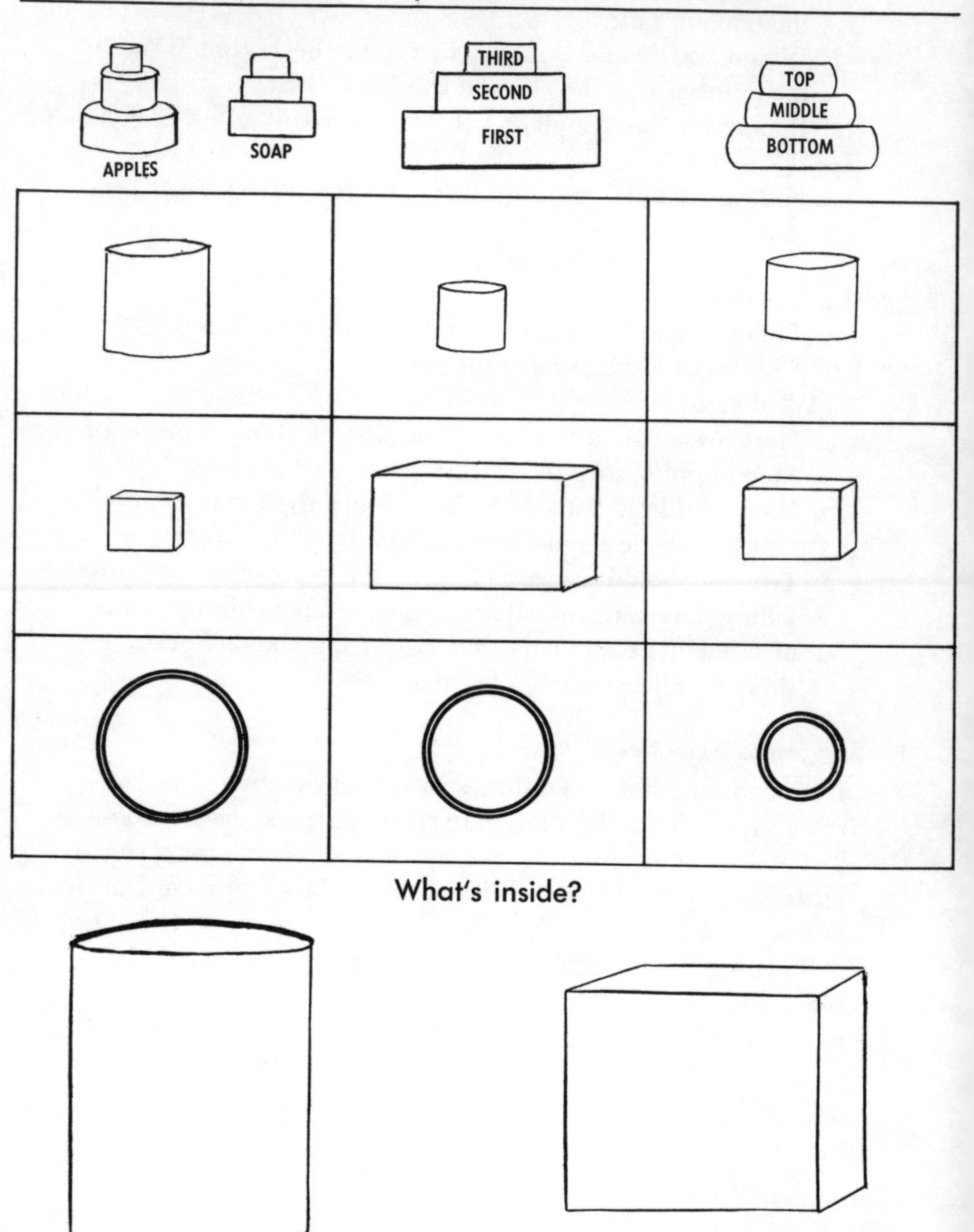

What's inside?

A. Problem 9

How do labels help you?

B. Materials

A sealed box or carton (cord or tape). Write signs on the box – HANDLE WITH CARE, OPEN HERE, THIS END UP, UP ↑ Flash cards for signs.

C. Method

1. Questions
   a. Did the mailman ever bring a box (package) to your house? What was in it?
   b. Encourage children to tell their experiences.
2. Display box
   a. Teacher: I have a box on this table. (Place box so that signs are upside down.) What do you think is in it? (Place flash cards in the box during preparation of materials. The children will find them when the box is opened.)
   b. Encourage children to look at the box to discover if they see something wrong with the way the box has been put on the table. How do you know that the box is upside down? (By the lettering.) Can you find the word that tells you how . . . ? (THIS END UP ↑) Provide information if children do not.
   c. Discuss the meaning of HANDLE WITH CARE (FRAGILE, GLASS, DO NOT DROP). What could happen if you are not careful with the box? What could happen if you dropped the box?
   d. Can you open the box? Discuss OPEN HERE (OPEN AT THIS END).
   e. What tool would you use to open the box? (Scissors to cut the cord or tape. Discuss safety factor.)
3. Flash cards
   Open the box. Children will discover the word cards. Remove flash cards that are in the box. Have children match the cards to the same word written on the box as a drill exercise. Use the cards for other word matching games.

D. Solution

1. Labels give information regarding how to place a box or carton.

2. Labels give information regarding the contents of a package.

3. Labels give information regarding how to open a box, carton or package.

4. Different objects can be sent by mail.

E. Learning Aids and Environmental Vocabulary

1. Shapes of boxes or cartons
2. Arrows – UP ↑ DOWN ↓
3. Labels – HANDLE WITH CARE, THIS END UP, OPEN HERE, etc.

F. Related Problems

1. How do you pack or place objects in a carton?
2. What is the procedure for sending packages by mail?
3. How do department stores pack and deliver packages?
4. How do neighborhood stores (grocery, paint, hardware, etc.) pack and deliver their products?

G. Teacher Directions

Problem Worksheet No. 9

1. Review words on problem worksheet.
2. Direct children's attention to the box pictured on problem worksheet.
3. Have children draw a line between the labels that are the same.
4. Review directions orally.
5. The children pretend that a box has been delivered to their house.
   a. They may write appropriate signs on the box pictured on problem worksheet.
   b. They may draw a picture of what they think is inside the box.
   c. Encourage those children who are able to write stories (utilizing vocabulary) related to the problem. Example: What's in the box?
6. Information – discuss procedure, purpose.
   a. FROM (sender's name)
   b. TO (receiver's name)
   c. Provide additional lessons related to parcels.

H. Suggested Activities

1. What other signs can you find? (Signs related to the problem.) For example, FRAGILE, DO NOT DROP, etc.
2. Provide experience in packing objects of different sizes, shapes, materials. Encourage monitorial duties related to school service.
3. Visit a post office. How do you mail a package? (PARCEL POST). Write out rules. Examples: package size, tying, etc.
4. Vocational skills: work areas related to packing and unpacking. Examples: factory work, shipping clerk. Encourage children to help at home.

No. 9 How do labels help you?

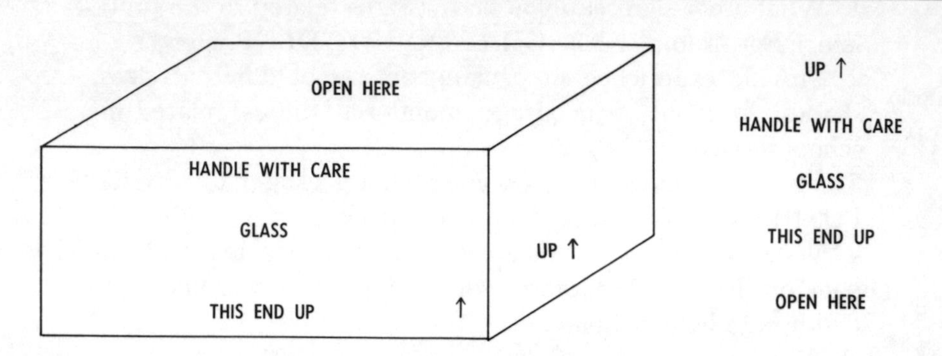

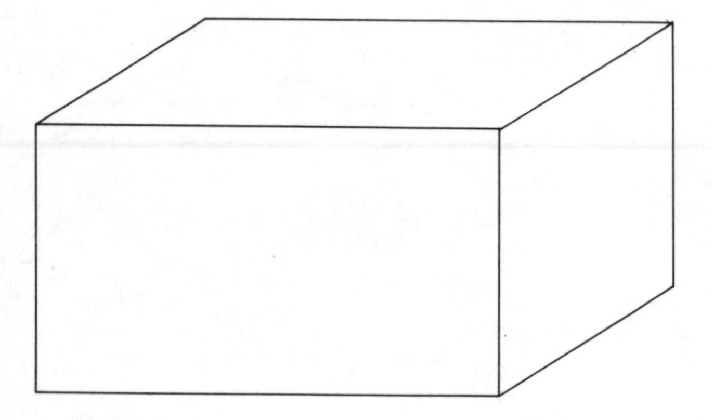

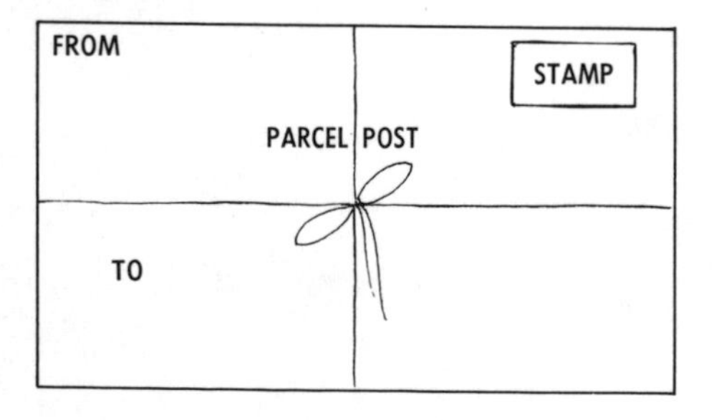

A. Problem 10

<u>How can you fit them together?</u>

B. Materials

Box, jar, bag, pots, pans (with covers), objects or pictures of key and lock, letter and mailbox, bread and toaster.

C. Method

1. Experiment A: Which ones belong together?
   a. Place a variety of objects on a table before the group: boxes (shoebox, eggbox, breadbox), jars and bottles (varied types and covers), pots and pans (varied types and covers).
   b. Have children match the covers that fit the appropriate jars, bottles, pots and pans. How do they fit together? Develop the concept that some objects belong together (fit), and are used for storing or protecting things? Why should we put on the right cover?
   c. Match eggs with eggbox, shoes with shoebox, etc. Why?
2. Experiment B: What fits in here?
   a. Use pictures or objects – key and lock, plug and outlet, bread and toaster, letter and mailbox.
   b. Again have children match appropriate objects. Would you put a key in the toaster? Develop the concept that some objects have openings to perform a function (to help us). For example, we put a key into the lock to open the door. We put a slice of bread into the toaster to. . . . Would you put a box in the mailbox slot (opening)? What fits in? (Envelopes, LETTERS, postcards.) Why?
3. Related situations
   a. Bags: Display a variety of different size bags. What do you put in a bag? What happens when you put in too much? How do you pick it up?
   b. Money slots: COIN machines such as CANDY, SODA, MILK, TELEPHONE. Also vehicles (BUS, TRAIN). Which COIN do you put into the slot? 5¢, 10¢, 25¢? What tells you how much to put into the machine? How does it fit?
   c. Clothes: hats, dresses, pants, shoes. How do they fit?

Does your foot hurt? How do you know it fits? What is your size?

d. Other openings: hose and hydrant, hose and vacuum cleaner, hose and air or gasoline pump.

4. Review

a. Review each experiment.

b. Discuss each situation.

c. Place objects and word cards on display. Encourage children to manipulate, handle and experiment with objects during free activities period. (Which one fits? Example: pots and covers.) Give further opportunity for similar experiences by providing puzzles and other manipulative toys or games that relate to concepts developed in lesson.

D. Conclusion

1. We know that some objects belong together (match or fit) because of their shapes (pot and cover).

2. We know that some objects belong together because of their function (key and lock).

3. We know that some objects belong together because of their size (foot and shoe).

4. In our environment there are many objects that fit into openings, slots, or holes (COINS, LETTERS, hose and hydrant).

E. Learning Aids and Environmental Vocabulary

1. Concept: Some objects belong together. We do not force objects to fit together. Observe their size, shape, function, name, location, etc.

2. Vocabulary: related to aspects of problem — size, slot, shoebox, lock, hose, etc.

3. Signs

a. BAG

b. BOX

c. CARTON

d. Objects: LETTERS, COINS, SHOES, POTS, etc.

e. JAR, POTS, PANS

F. Related Problems

1. What safety rules should you follow regarding filling containers, boxes, bags or jars?
2. Should you put your hands or fingers into unfamiliar openings, holes or slots?
3. Why is size important? Examples: bulb and fuse, sock and foot.
4. Why is it important to return objects to the places they belong (soap to soapdish, clothes to hanger, toothbrush to holder, telephone to hook)?

G. Teacher Directions

Problem Worksheet No. 10

1. Use poem to review problem. Read aloud to class or write on blackboard. Mount as a chart.
2. Exercise: Which ones belong together? Find 2!
   a. Discuss pictures or objects that belong or fit together.
   b. Place word cards (labels) on pictures and objects.
   c. Instruct children to match objects. Example: Draw a line. . . .
   d. Encourage group to add other objects that belong together. Example: LETTERS and mailbox, plug and outlet, hose and vacuum cleaner.
   e. Children may write their own labels by copying signs written on objects.

H. Suggested Activities

1. Construct a chart depicting objects that belong together according to size, shape, function. Develop rules for using each correctly. Write a summary of the demonstrations.
2. Vocational skills
   a. How to fill bags, boxes, jars, etc.
   b. How to lift and carry a bag or carton. Dangers in carrying trays that are too heavy.
   c. DELIVERIES: RING BELL, USE BACK DOOR, SIDE ENTRANCE, BEWARE OF DOG.
   d. What kind of bag would you use for dairy products, canned foods, etc.?

3. Mathematics
   a. Relate sizes and shapes to clothes, food and household objects.
   b. Explain units of measure – SIZES, yards, etc.
   c. Have students make booklets containing different sizes and shapes (big and small, round and square).
4. Other demonstrations related to problem
   a. How to use a water hose or air pump.
   b. How to refill a stapler.
   c. How to put a pillow into a pillowcase. (How to fold blankets and quilts.)
   d. How to thread a needle.
   e. How to use a coin-operated machine (telephone, candy).

No. 10 How can you fit them together?

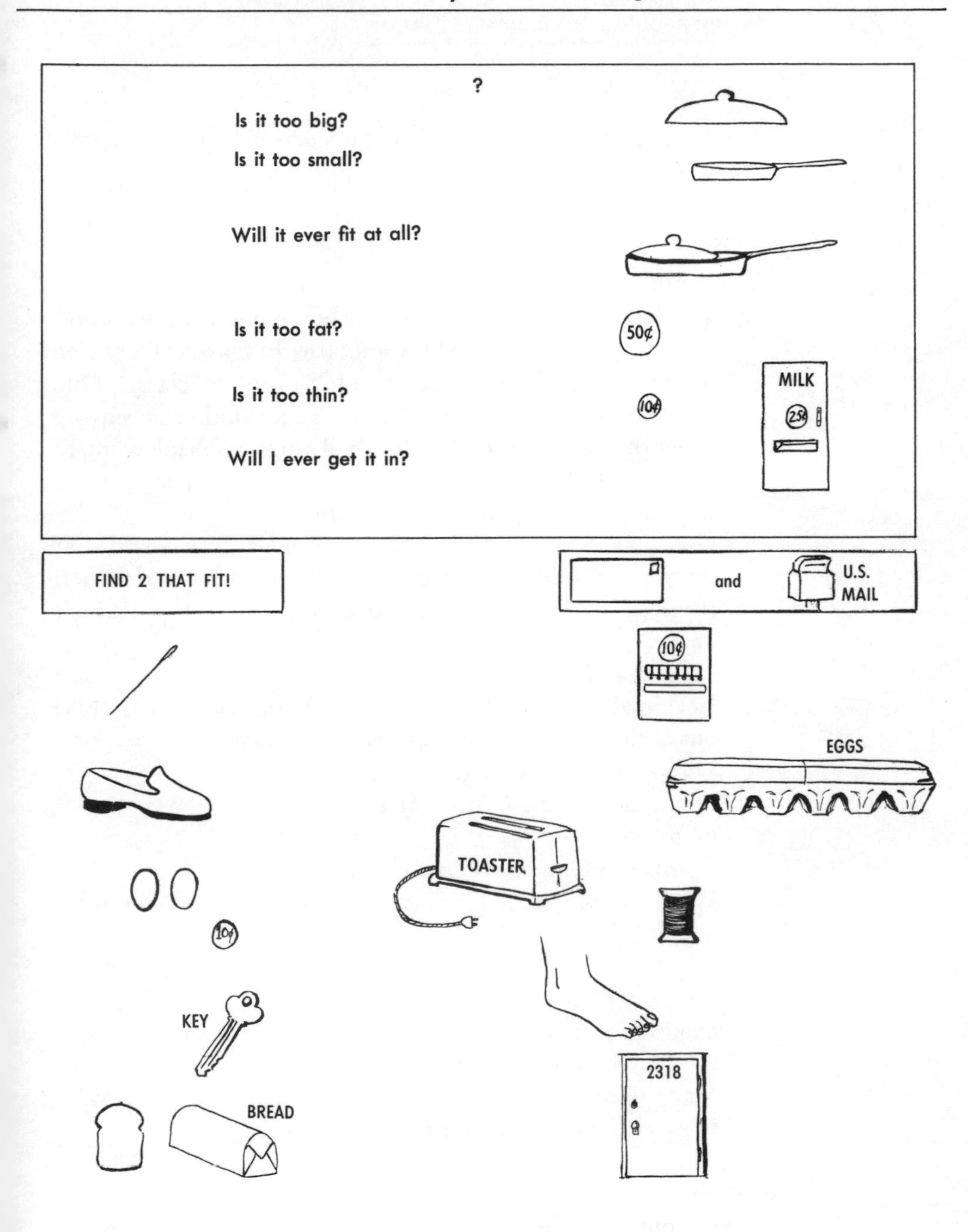

A. Problem 11

When should you open your door?

B. Materials

Magazine pictures: one boy, one girl, private house or apartment house.

C. Method

1. Situation
   a. Teacher: Here is a picture of a boy named Michael and a girl named Susan. (Show pictures to class.) They live in this house. (Show picture of "house" to class.) One day they were alone in the house. Their mother was away at work. They heard the doorbell ring. Michael went to the door and opened it. Susan was angry. "You did the wrong thing, Michael," said Susan.
   b. Question: Should Michael have opened the door? What do you do when you are home alone and the doorbell rings? Would you open the door for someone you don't know?
2. Dramatization
   a. Let's make believe that we are at home. Send one child out of the room. Choose another child to answer the door.
   b. Discuss the safe way to answer the door.
   c. Dramatize "Who is it?" "It is (name)."
3. Discussion
   a. Emphasize politeness to strangers, not fear.
   b. What would you do if someone wants to leave a "sample" or gift?
   c. When can you let people come into your home? When, for example, Mother tells you that . . . the janitor is coming to fix the sink, the grocery boy will deliver food, the mailman will bring a package, etc.
   d. Many different people come to our houses – friends, relatives, delivery men, community helpers, etc.

D. Solution

1. Be polite but firm in not allowing strangers into your homes. We always ask, "Who is it?"

2. Open the door to familiar friends, neighbors and relatives. We do not open the door to strangers.
3. Accept packages and gifts on parents' instructions.
4. Welcome a community helper whom you were told to expect, or if an emergency occurs.

E. Learning Aids and Environmental Vocabulary

1. Learn the names of different friends, relatives and helpers.
2. Recognize uniforms of different community helpers.
3. Associate tools used with work performed by different helpers.
4. "Who is it?" Names: MILKMAN, LAUNDRY MAN, DELIVERY BOY, MAILMAN, etc.

F. Related Problems

1. Should you accept candy or money from strangers?
2. Should you accept car rides from strangers?
3. Are you familiar with (do you know) other people in your house and neighborhood?
4. Are you polite and friendly with people you know?
5. Do you practice good manners? (Hello. Goodbye.)

G. Teacher Directions

Problem Worksheet No. 11

1. Discussion
   a. Many people come to your house. Some are friends, neighbors or relatives. Do you know their names? Who are they? (Encourage children's participation in discussion. Emphasize positive and friendly social relationships.)
2. Worksheet instructions
   a. Many community helpers or workers come to your house. There are different ways to know who they are. How? (Names or titles, uniforms, tools they use, services they perform.) Let's find out how many you know.
   b. Have children give name of each helper pictured at the top of the problem worksheet.
   c. Discuss the colors of the uniforms (clothes) each one wears. Emphasize familiar associations.
   d. Discuss the services each performs. (What does he do to help you?)

e. Discuss the tools or object identified with each helper.
f. Direct children's attention to problem worksheet instructions. Who is it? (Write each name under each picture.) What does he do? What does he use? (Draw a line from object to helper.) What does he wear? (Color his clothes or uniform appropriately: Fireman – red, Mailman – blue, etc.)

H. Suggested Activities

1. Dramatize other situations related to the problem. Encourage children to discuss their own experiences.
2. Discuss and record rules to follow related to the problem.
3. Stress good manners – making introductions, taking messages, etc.
4. Plan a unit of study on the different workers and helpers at school, home and community. Stress appreciation of job duties.
5. Construct similar problem worksheets utilizing other helpers such as carpenters, plumbers, etc.

No. 11 When should you open your door?

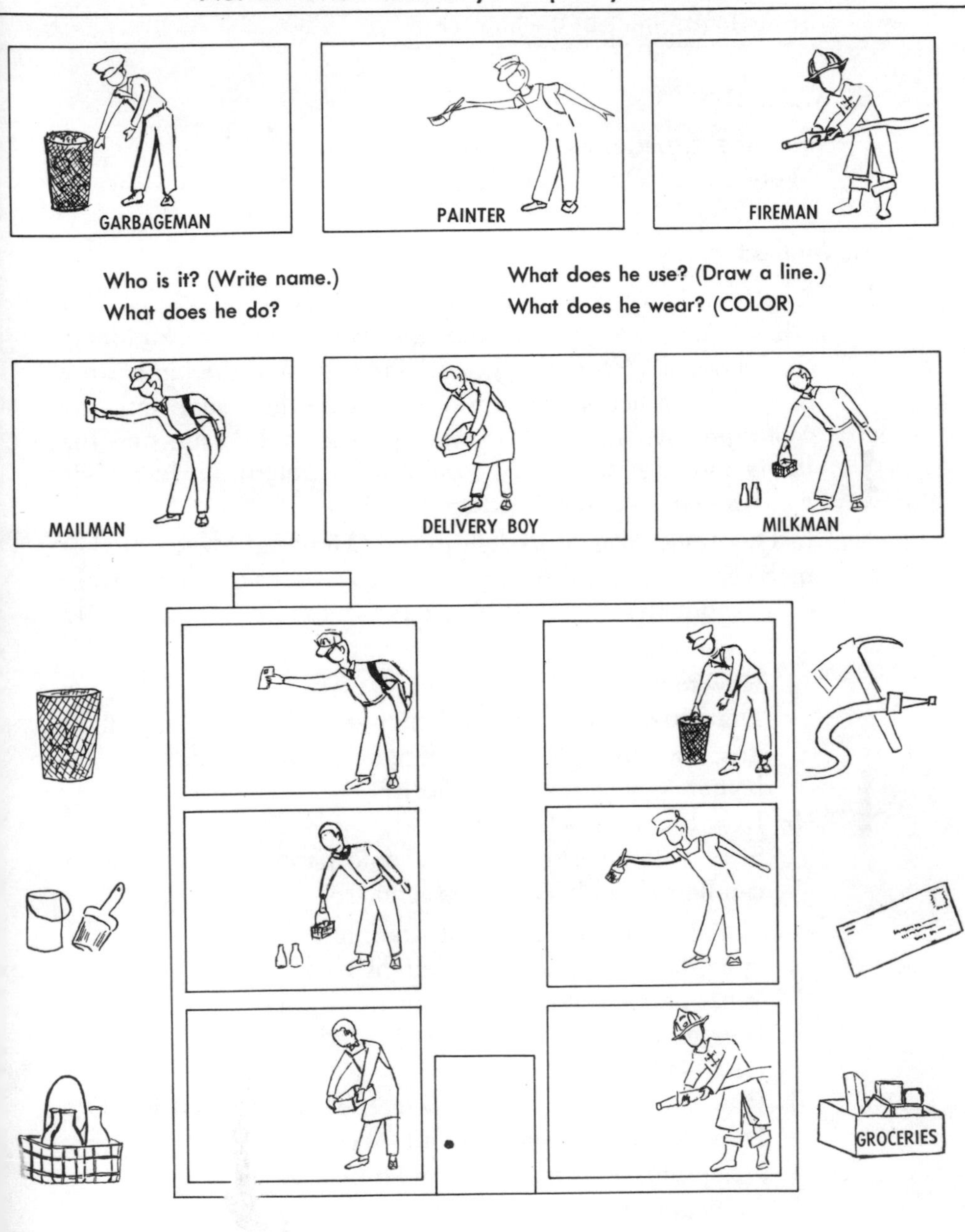

Who is it? (Write name.)
What does he do?

What does he use? (Draw a line.)
What does he wear? (COLOR)

A. Problem 12

How do different lights help you?

B. Materials

Flashlight, batteries, light switch, cord with plug.
Word cards: ON and OFF, FLASHLIGHT, CANDLES

C. Method

1. Story: Mary was in her house watching television. Her whole family was at home too. Everyone was busy. Suddenly the television picture was gone! Mary saw that the lights were out too. The house was dark. Mary's mother came into the room quickly. "Don't worry, Mary," she said. "I am sure the lights and television will be on in a few minutes. Meanwhile we can make our own lights!" How?
2. Questions: Was Mary frightened? How did Mary's mother make her own lights? What would you do if your lights went OFF suddenly?
3. Demonstrations
   a. How to use a FLASHLIGHT
   Dramatize situation. Darken room. Does the flashlight give enough light in an emergency? Do you have one at home? Where do you keep it?
   b. How to use CANDLES
   Stress safety factor. Adults should handle candles! Use a candlestick for greater protection.
4. Related situations for demonstration
   a. How do you replace a flashlight battery?
   b. What happens when you "put in" a plug?
   c. How do you use a wall (electric) light switch? OFF – ON
   d. How do you use a lamp (electric) switch? OFF – ON
   e. Directional lights on cars and bicycles
   f. Headlights on cars, trucks and other vehicles
5. People (helpers)
   a. Man who checks the electric meter. Who is he? When does he come? What does he do?
   b. Repair man
   c. Who changes fuses in your house?

d. Store: where would you buy BATTERIES, FLASH-LIGHT, LIGHT BULB?

6. Summary: how electric lights help us
   a. Hallway and doorway lights
   b. Lampposts in streets
   c. Road lights
   d. Electric lighting in stores, buildings and public places
   e. Nightlights in the home

D. Solution

1. We have lamps and overhead electric lights in our homes to help us see.
2. When it is dark, we switch ON the lights.
3. During the day we switch OFF the lights. The sun gives us light.
4. The streets, buildings and stores are lit in many ways.

E. Learning Aids and Environmental Vocabulary

1. Concepts
   a. Electric lights help to keep us safe when it is dark. Examples: street and hallway lights.
   b. Electric lights help us enjoy activities at night. We can read and play games although it is dark.
   c. There are other ways of creating light. Examples: flash-lights, candles.
2. Vocabulary: BATTERIES, switch, lamppost, traffic lights, etc.
3. Signs
   a. ON – OFF
   b. Traffic lights: STOP (red light), GO (green light), WAIT (yellow light)
   c. LIGHT BULB

F. Related Problems

1. What does a flashing or blinking light mean? Examples: ambulance or police car.
2. How do you change a fuse? Who should . . . ?
3. Should you loiter in dark or unlit hallways? On the street?
4. Who helps you in other emergency situations? What would you do?

G. Teacher Directions

Problem Worksheet No. 12

1. Utilize worksheet poems to review concepts.
   a. How lights help us at home
   b. How lights help us in the street
2. Read each aloud.
   a. Discuss meanings.
   b. Review vocabulary ON, OFF, etc.
   c. Write poems, illustrate, display as charts. Encourage children's contributions of drawings or pictures for each category (home and street).
3. Write words on blackboard. Also use word cards.
   a. ON – OFF
   b. FLASHLIGHT (BATTERIES, BULB)
   c. Colors of traffic lights
   d. Signs associated with traffic lights: STOP, GO, WAIT, WALK, DO NOT WALK
4. Children may complete each sentence orally or fill in correct word.
5. Encourage children to think of other signs and to write original sentences.

H. Suggested Activities

1. Vocational skills: learn the names and functions of switches, plugs, switch plate, extension cord. Stress those skills necessary for daily living. Examples: how to pull out a plug or cord, how to locate switches on electric appliances or other objects in the home – TV set, lamps.
2. Visit a store where equipment is sold. Compile a list of signs noted: LIGHT BULBS, WATT, CLEAR, TINTED. (Could you go on an errand?)
3. Safety rules related to the problem
   a. Dangers of electricity
   b. Using switches, plugs, etc., correctly
   c. How nightlights help us
   d. Observe traffic lights
   e. Bicycle and car lights should be used at night.
4. Behavior in emergency situations. Who would help you?
   a. Neighbor
   b. Building custodian (janitor, superintendent)

c. Police and fire departments
d. How to use the phone in an emergency (OPERATOR, AMBULANCE, FIRE DEPT., POLICE DEPT.)
e. There are many people who will help you!

No. 12 How do different lights help you?

?

OFF FLASHLIGHT WALK ON WAIT

1. When I want light I push ____________.
2. Before I go to sleep I turn my lamp ____.
3. When the light is yellow I ____________.
4. When the light is green I ____________.
5. It is fun to use a ____________.

A. Problem 13

Why do you use SOAP?

B. Materials

Soap, water, washcloth, two basins, and article of clothing
Signs: SELF-SERVICE LAUNDRY, SOAP, WATER, WASH, DRY

C. Method

1. Experiment
   a. Set up two basins of water.
   b. Child washes hands using water only.
   c. Child washes hands using soap and water.
   d. Compare. Which water is dirtier? Whose hands are cleaner?
   e. Repeat the demonstration using a washcloth. (Note the dirt on the washcloth.)
   f. Repeat the demonstration using an article of clothing.
2. Discuss home laundering.
   a. Do you help mother wash clothes?
   b. Where does your mother wash the clothes (sink, washing machine)?
   c. How does your mother wash the clothes? (Uses hands, machine.)
3. Story: The Self-Service Laundry

   Susan's mother heard about a wonderful place where she could have the family's clothes washed and dried. Of course, it did cost money, but Susan's mother thought she would like to see how they wash the clothes and how much it cost.

   They walked for a little while, and then came to a store. Mother said, "This is the place!" Over the doorway was a sign that said SELF-SERVICE LAUNDRY (show sign to children). They opened the door and walked in. What did they see? What was happening in the LAUNDRY?
4. Signs

   Susan and her mother saw many signs in the LAUNDRY. They told Susan and her mother how to use the LAUNDRY. Teacher may write signs on the blackboard, use flash cards, or the problem worksheet chart to discuss meaning and vocabulary. What does SELF-SERVICE mean? (AUTOMATIC?)

D. Solution

1. Soap helps to keep our bodies clean.
2. Soap helps to clean our clothes.
3. Water does not clean as well as soap. Soap removes dirt better than water.
4. Machines do jobs that save us time and effort. (Example: washing machines)

E. Learning Aids and Environmental Vocabulary

1. SELF-SERVICE LAUNDRY
2. SOAP
3. WATER
4. WASH
5. DRY

F. Related Problems

1. Does HOT or COLD water remove dirt better?
2. Why should you wash your hair, take baths and showers?
3. Why should members of the family have their own wash-cloths and towels?
4. What other machines help to keep our families and homes clean? (Vacuum cleaners, etc.)
5. What other SELF-SERVICE stores do you know? (SU-PERMARKET, etc.)

G. Teacher Directions

Problem Worksheet No. 13

1. Chart
   a. Use chart to develop steps in using SELF-SERVICE LAUNDRY. Discuss signs and meanings.
   b. Have children note the signs to the left of each sentence of instructions. For example: [COINS] Put COINS here.
   c. Instruct children to draw a line under the same word when they find it in the sentence. Example: [COINS] Put <u>COINS</u> here.

2. OTHER STORES

a. Other stores perform services that help to keep us clean and neat.
b. Look at the row of stores. How many do you know? How do they help us?
c. Discuss each store and the service it performs.
d. Instruct children to draw a line from the name of the store to the picture and sentence that tells how the store helps us. Read each sentence.
e. Look at the names of each store. Write the correct name over each doorway. Do this exercise with the class. Example:

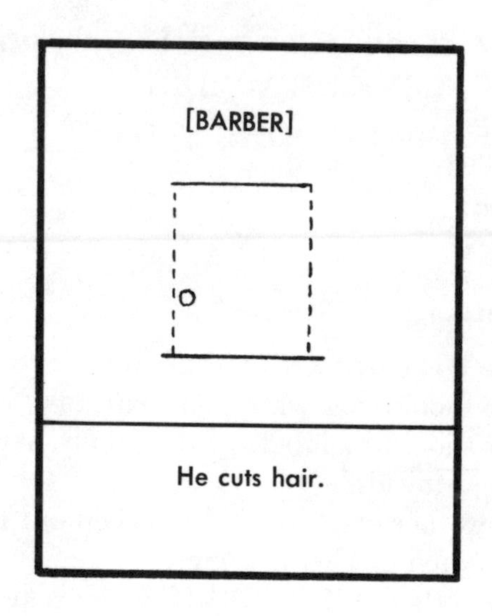

H. Suggested Activities

1. Visit a laundry, barbershop, cleaners, etc. Develop an appreciation of different types of jobs and work.
2. Keep room clean. Wash shelves, desks, equipment. Use soap. Why?
3. Mathematics: money – amount needed to wash clothes. Price lists: cleaners, tailor, etc.
4. Discuss safety rules regarding use of detergents, cleaning fluids, etc. (covers, vapors, spray cans).
5. We should learn to use appliances related to keeping our clothes clean. Examples: washing machine, dryer, iron, etc.

No. 13 Why do you use SOAP?

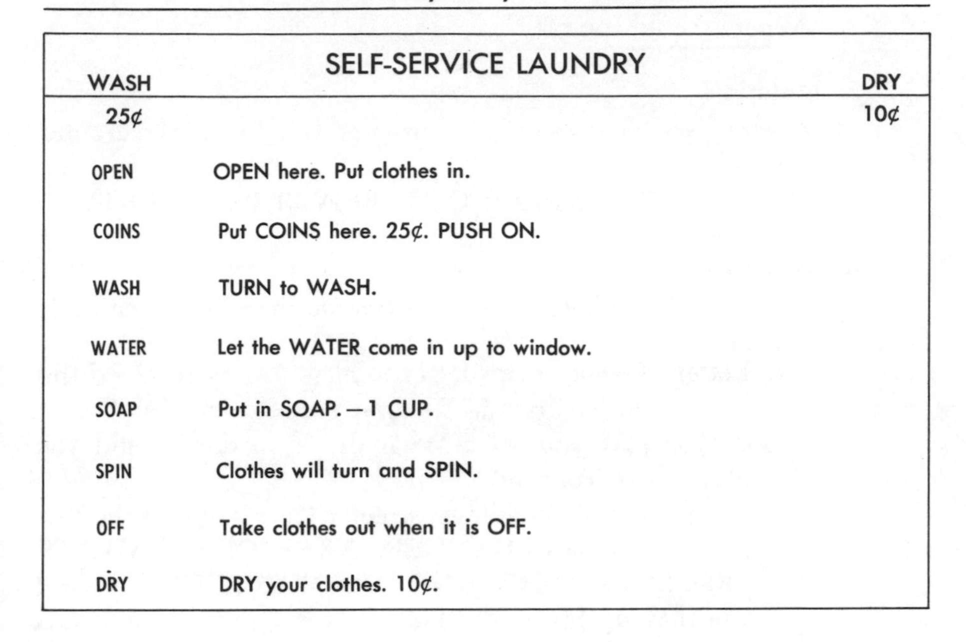

WASH	SELF-SERVICE LAUNDRY	DRY
25¢		10¢
OPEN	OPEN here. Put clothes in.	
COINS	Put COINS here. 25¢. PUSH ON.	
WASH	TURN to WASH.	
WATER	Let the WATER come in up to window.	
SOAP	Put in SOAP. — 1 CUP.	
SPIN	Clothes will turn and SPIN.	
OFF	Take clothes out when it is OFF.	
DRY	DRY your clothes. 10¢.	

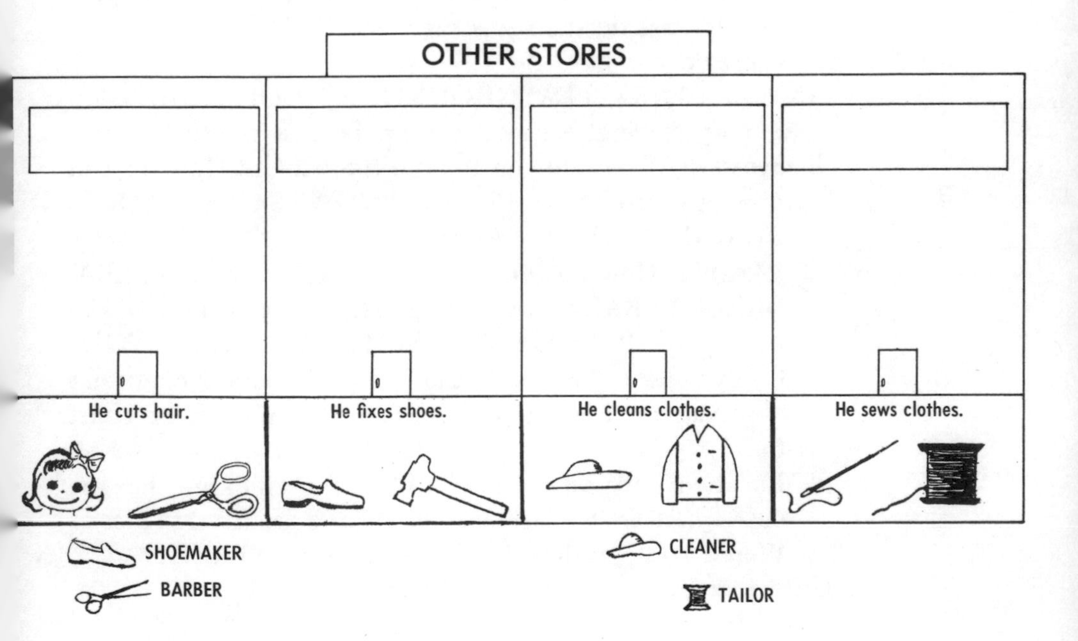

A. Problem 14

Where should you play?

B. Materials

Letter (see worksheet), pictures of buildings, playground, streets

Signs: DANGER, KEEP OUT, PRIVATE PROPERTY

C. Method

1. Would you play here? The situation may be presented in one of the following ways:
   a. Letter: Teacher reads letter to class. "Mary received this letter from her friend." Do you write to friends? Where do you play outdoors? What did Tom do? Would you play where Tom did? Why?
   b. Use pictures of buildings, streets: Paste signs on the pictures. Examples: DANGER, KEEP OUT, PRIVATE PROPERTY, DEAD END, DO NOT ENTER. Would you play in this empty house? Is it safe to go into this building? How do you know that it is not safe to play here? What do the signs say?
2. Where do you play?
   a. Places: PARK, PLAYGROUND, SCHOOL YARD, community or neighborhood center. Discuss safety factors.
   b. Seasons: Where do you play in the winter? How do you protect yourself from ICE and SNOW? Summer? POOL, BEACH.
   c. Weather: How do you protect yourself in the rain? UMBRELLA, RAINCOAT, RAINHAT. How do BOOTS help you? PAVEMENT – SLIPPERY WHEN WET. Can you see or be seen in the FOG? Encourage children's observations. Record observations in a picture or chart form.
   d. Location: city or country? Why is hitchhiking dangerous? KEEP OFF –THIN ICE. What does this sign mean? Would you play here? What is a PLAY STREET?
3. Review and summarize concepts developed in the lesson.

D. Solution

1. It is safe to play in the PARK, PLAYGROUND, SCHOOL

YARD or neighborhood community center.

2. We should be careful on snowy and rainy days.

3. Safety rules should be followed in public places (PLAYGROUND, BEACH, POOL).

4. Children should not play in empty buildings or warehouses. Signs tell us where it is safe to play.

E. Learning Aids and Environmental Vocabulary

1. Concept: DANGER – KEEP OUT
2. Vocabulary: PARK, PLAY STREET, SCHOOL YARD
3. Signs
   a. Buildings – PRIVATE PROPERTY
   b. Places – BEACH, POOL, PLAYGROUND
   c. Things – SWINGS, BOOTS, BALL, and other play equipment

F. Related Problems

1. Why are streets and roads slippery when it rains or snows?
2. Should you play outdoors when it is night? (Dark?)
3. How do you know when it is time to come home?
4. Do you run better when you wear sneakers or heavy boots?

G. Teacher Directions

Problem Worksheet No. 14

1. Review or read the worksheet letter aloud.
2. Discuss the situation.
   a. Friends: What are the names of your friends? What games do you enjoy playing? Do you play at home with your friends?
   b. Where do you play in your neighborhood? Where is the PLAYGROUND? PARK?
   c. What did Tom do? Would you play in . . . ?
3. Letter: Instruct children to put a green line under places that are safe to play.
4. Where do you play?
   a. Read names in column. Questions.
   b. Check or write YES or NO after each.
   c. Children write names of other places in which they can play. Example: GYM, COMMUNITY CENTER.

5. Do you look?
   a. Read signs in the column.
   b. What other signs do you see that help to keep you safe when you play? Children write additional signs: NO LOITERING, KEEP OFF, etc.

6. Provide additional experience in letter writing. Children may draw pictures to tell a story (picture letters).

H. Suggested Activities

1. Plan a unit of study to topic: PLAY.
   a. Play equipment: TOYS, GAMES, BAT and BALL
   Use: Why should you wear a glove when you catch a baseball?
   b. People who help us: playground worker, group leader, POLICEMAN, park attendant, teacher, friends and parents
   c. Play and health: seasonal play, exercise, rest, activity. Rules and regulations.
2. Experiments
   a. Why should you wear boots and raincoat? (Materials: plastic and rubber.) Soak a shoe and a boot in water. Which is dry?
   b. Compare running in shoes, boots and sneakers. Which is easiest?
   c. Why is it dangerous to walk in front of a swing, between the batter and the catcher?
3. Relate time, weather and season to the topic.
   a. When do you come in? Time: clock, night, dark. Days are longer in summer.
   b. We wear appropriate playclothes for each season and in different kinds of weather (heavy and light clothing).
   c. Temperature: thermometer, COLD, COOL, HOT, BELOW ZERO

4. Children list and illustrate signs IN THE COUNTRY and IN THE CITY.

No. 14 Where should you play?

May 1, 19____

Dear Mary,

It is raining. I am in my house. I play in the house on rainy days. I play ball on sunny days. I go to the PARK and the PLAYGROUND. I have fun in the SCHOOL YARD. I know when to go home. I always come in when it is dark! One day Tom played here.

I know where to play!

DANGER
KEEP OUT
PRIVATE
PROPERTY

Come to see me. We will play and have fun.

Your friend,

Bob

Where do you play?	Do you look?
1. PARK	1. DANGER
2. PLAYGROUND	2. KEEP OUT
3. SCHOOL YARD	3. PRIVATE PROPERTY
4. PLAY STREET	4. NO TRESPASSING
5. ____________	5. ______________

A. Problem 15

What should you do when you ride and travel?

B. Materials

Wagon, doll, blocks
Signs: SAFETY BELT, SCHOOL BUS, CAR

C. Method

1. Discussion: Introduce the topic with a discussion on the different ways to travel.
Questions: How do you come to school? Do you ride a bicycle? How do you go from place to place in the city? Do you enjoy riding in a car?
2. Experiment A: Should you stand or sit down in the SCHOOL BUS?
  a. Use a small wagon as the SCHOOL BUS (sign). Have children place 3 or 4 tall blocks in the wagon. Pull the wagon slowly at first. Bring the wagon to an abrupt stop.
  b. Questions: What happened to the blocks? Why did they fall? Which way did the blocks fall? Did they fall back?
  c. Repeat experiment by putting blocks flat on their broad sides. Use a doll to demonstrate that sitting down is safer than standing in a moving vehicle. Relate to children's own experiences in the BUS.
3. Experiment B: How do SAFETY BELTS help to keep you safe?
  a. Use the doll (in a sitting position) as a passenger. Pull the wagon (CAR) slowly. Again bring the wagon to an abrupt halt. What happened to the doll?
  b. SAFETY BELTS keep us safe. Repeat the experiment with a belt or rope. (Attach it to wagon and around the doll.) Did the doll fall this time? Do you wear a SAFETY BELT when you ride in a car? Why?
4. Related situations
  a. Where do you wait? (BUS STOP, TAXI STAND, etc.)
  b. Where is it safe to stand on a train platform?
  c. Should you "hitch" rides on the back of buses or trucks? Demonstrate by using doll and toy truck.
  d. What signs and signals do you see when you ride? (Traffic signs, directional signals, etc.) Dramatize a ride.

D. Conclusion

1. It is safer to sit when riding in a moving vehicle.
2. Safety belts keep us from falling when the car stops suddenly.
3. It is dangerous to "hitch" rides on the backs of vehicles.
4. We should observe and read the signs (and signals) that help to keep us safe when we travel.

E. Learning Aids and Environmental Vocabulary

1. Vocabulary: CAR, BUS, TRUCK, TRAIN, TAXI, BICYCLE, SAFETY BELT
2. Signals: traffic lights, directionals on vehicles, hand signals
3. Signs
   a. BUS STOP, SCHOOL BUS
   b. FULL STOP
   c. TAXI STAND, TRAIN PLATFORM
   d. TRUCKS ONLY

F. Related Problems

1. What rules do you observe when you ride your bicycle?
2. Should you distract (annoy) the driver when you are riding in a bus, car, train, etc.?
3. How do wheels help us?
4. How do the different service people help? (Gasoline station attendant, garage mechanic, taxi and bus drivers.)

G. Teacher Directions

Problem Worksheet No. 15

1. Review each experiment emphasizing the safety signs and regulations related to the problem.
2. Read the worksheet safety rules related to:
   a. SCHOOL BUS
   b. BICYCLE
   c. CAR
3. Instruct children to draw lines under the words that are the same. Example: SCHOOL BUS – I always sit down in the SCHOOL BUS. Encourage individual responses. Children may write additional rules in each box. Example: I help the BUS DRIVER.
4. "I ride. I LOOK. Do you?" (Problem worksheet.)

What signs do you see when you ride . . . ? (Dramatize.) Children write signs related to riding, travel, traffic, regulations, etc. (NO STANDING – BUS STOP, GARAGE, CAR WASH, PARK HERE, NO BICYCLING, USE BICYCLE PATH, DRIVE SLOWLY).

H. Suggested Activities

1. Visit a GARAGE, SERVICE STATION, BICYCLE REPAIR SHOP.
2. Vocational skills
   a. Duties of helper in a CAR WASH station
   b. How to keep a car and bicycle clean
   c. Duties of the parking lot attendant (take tickets, watchman)
3. Plan a unit of study related to the problem.
   a. Different ways of getting around the city
   b. People who help us in the community. Drivers – BUS, TRUCK, TAXI
   c. Places related to the topic: GARAGE (REPAIRS), PARKING LOT (MAN ON DUTY), SERVICE STATION (GASOLINE), BUS DEPOT
4. Dramatize situations to emphasize safety regulations. Children may construct puppets.
   a. Traffic lights and signs
   b. Where should you wait? Corners, behavior at BUS STOP, courtesy, waiting your turn.
   c. How to use a SAFETY BELT
   d. How to behave in a SERVICE STATION or GARAGE (DANGER)

No. 15 What should you do when you ride and travel?

WAIT	I WAIT for the BUS.
SCHOOL BUS	I always sit down in the SCHOOL BUS.
DO NOT TOUCH	I DO NOT TOUCH the DOORS.

BICYCLE	I ride my BICYCLE near my house.
STOP - GO	I look for STOP and GO.
LIGHTS	I have LIGHTS and a horn.

CAR	I ride in a CAR.
SAFETY BELT	I wear my SAFETY BELT.
PASS LEFT	We PASS on the LEFT.

I ride.	I LOOK!	Do you?

A. **Problem 16**

How should you handle an animal?

B. **Materials**

Signs: ZOO, CIRCUS, PET STORE, CURB YOUR DOG, NO PETS ALLOWED, DO NOT FEED ANIMALS, KEEP HANDS OFF

C. **Method**

1. Situation A: PETS
   a. Teacher: Tommy loved dogs. He liked to touch them. Tommy liked to feel the soft fur. (Do you?) One day, Tommy was playing in the street. He saw a beautiful dog! The owner was walking with his dog. Tommy stopped playing and ran to the dog. He bent over quickly and began to hug the dog. The man who was with the dog (the owner) said: "STOP! Please don't touch the dog." Why?
   b. Questions: What should Tommy have done? Was the dog afraid? Should Tommy have asked the man if he could touch the dog? Should you play with strange animals? Why?
2. Situation B: WILD ANIMALS
   a. Teacher: Tommy went to the ZOO. (Show children sign.) He was very happy to be there. Again, he forgot what he should do. He ran up to the lions' cage and began throwing peanuts into the cage. He went behind the special gate and put his hands inside the cage. The man who takes care of the ZOO animals said: "STOP! Can't you read the signs?" (Show children 2 signs.) DO NOT FEED ANIMALS, KEEP HANDS OFF (cages).
   b. Questions: What did the signs say? Mean? What should Tommy have done? Why? What could happen if you don't do as the sign tells you?
3. Discussion
   a. Review the proper way to approach animals.
   b. How to behave at the ZOO or CIRCUS
   c. Discuss the responsibilities of owning a pet (leash, license, CURB YOUR DOG, NO PETS ALLOWED). Keep pets on a leash. Pets in apartment houses.

d. How to behave toward animals (treatment of pets, teasing)

D. Solution

1. We should not run up to (approach) strange animals.
2. We should always ask the owner if we may touch his pet.
3. We should be kind (gentle) to all animals.
4. Animals that live in cages (ZOO, CIRCUS) should not be touched or teased.

E. Learning Aids and Environmental Vocabulary

1. Signs: PETS
   a. CURB YOUR DOG
   b. PET STORE
   c. NO PETS ALLOWED
2. Signs: WILD ANIMALS
   a. ZOO – CIRCUS
   b. KEEP HANDS OFF
   c. DO NOT FEED ANIMALS

F. Related Problems

1. How do you care for your own PETS?
2. What is the job of the VETERINARIAN?
3. What is a dog license? Why does your dog need one?
4. What kinds of animals make good PETS?

G. Teacher Directions

Problem Worksheet No. 16

1. Review concepts developed in Situations A and B.
2. Dramatize each situation:
   a. How to approach an animal in the street
   b. How to approach an animal in the ZOO
3. Write each worksheet story on the blackboard (DOG – LION).
   a. Teacher or child reads story to class.
   b. Review signs included in each story. Use cards.
   c. Meaning of each sign
4. Children may write as many signs as they can, appropriate to each story (or situation). Use corrrect empty box. Others may draw a picture, write rules, or match signs to animal.

H. Suggested Activities

1. Visit a PET STORE or ZOO. Observe how the animals are handled. Write rules for handling and caring for animals in the home.
2. Craft activities – sew stuffed animals; construct wood projects involving different animal shapes. Leashes can be made from leather or plastic chains. Knit a coat or sweater for a dog or cat.
3. Plan a class PET SHOW (admission, tickets, sell craft projects).
4. Learn the rules and regulations related to owning a pet. Interview a pet store owner, veterinarian, dog catcher. What does a license cost? What medicine (injections – shots) does an animal need? What is the FINE for not walking your dog in the right place? (CURB YOUR DOG.)

No. 16 How should you handle an animal?

A. Problem 17

How do you hold an umbrella?

B. Materials

Umbrella, signs: THIN ICE, MEN AT WORK, KEEP OFF, STREET CLOSED, DETOUR

C. Method

1. Discussion
   a. Review the objects associated with protection from the rain (raincoat, hat, boots, umbrella).
   b. How do they help us? Discuss each.
   c. Review the names and functions of each part of an umbrella (top, handle).
2. Demonstration – how to hold an umbrella
   a. Use an umbrella or a large paper (oaktag) form.
   b. Ask children to pretend that it is raining.
   c. Choose a child to "walk" in the rain with his umbrella.
   d. Question class regarding how the child is holding the umbrella.
   e. Have another child hold the umbrella (low) so that the eyes are covered. Instruct child to walk and move. What do you think would happen if . . . ?
   f. Invite a child to hold the umbrella (high) above the eyes (head). Instruct child to walk and move. Why is this way better? Safer?
3. Concept: There are obstacle situations that the child meets daily. Our eyes help us to cope with these situations. Discuss, use pictures or demonstrations for the following:
   a. Swinging and revolving doors
   b. Ladders
   c. Delivery chutes (how cartons are delivered to stores)
   d. Swings
   e. Flying objects (balls, etc.)

D. Solution

1. Our eyes help to keep us safe from danger.
2. We hold an umbrella so that our eyes can help us to see where we are going.

3. There are many objects that protect us from the elements.
4. We understand the meaning of high and low.

E. Learning Aids and Environmental Vocabulary

1. Concept: LOOK – our eyes help us.
2. Names of objects associated with weather protection
3. Labels – UMBRELLA, RAINCOAT, RAINHAT, BOOTS
4. Obstacle situations – THIN ICE, MEN AT WORK, KEEP OFF, STREET CLOSED, DETOUR

F. Related Problems

1. Why are slippery or wet surfaces dangerous (water, ice)?
2. How would you handle other obstacle situations related to the problem? What are they?
3. How do you use sunglasses safely?
4. Why should you walk with your head up (posture)?

G. Teacher Directions

1. Use story on problem worksheet as a review of situation.
2. "I Look with My Eyes."
   a. Discuss each situation. Read signs aloud.
   b. Use word cards.
   c. Match the number and sign. Write number in box on picture.
   d. Develop concepts of around, over, on, off. (Example: Walk around the MEN AT WORK sign at open manhole.)
3. Encourage children to write and illustrate the signs in each situation. Children print the signs. What others have you seen?
4. Related discussions
   a. How to wear hats properly
   b. Fads: face shields, masks
   c. Behavior at a ball game or at the playground (flying objects)
   d. Meaning of "blocked" or "roped off" areas (DO NOT ENTER)

H. Suggested Activities

1. Unit of study on eyes: checkups, care of eyes, doctor, optician, foods that help the eyes, etc.
2. Develop a list of rules related to obstacle situations. Illustrate.
3. Teacher should examine children's eyes, place children at desks according to vision problems, encourage those children who wear glasses to use them, provide reading material that is in good condition (clear printing).
4. Signs and labels: Encourage children to locate words that relate to the problem. Add to child's list and word card set – DANGER, DETOUR, THIN ICE, KEEP OUT.
5. Mathematics concepts: high, low, on, off, around, over, under

No. 17 How do you hold an umbrella?

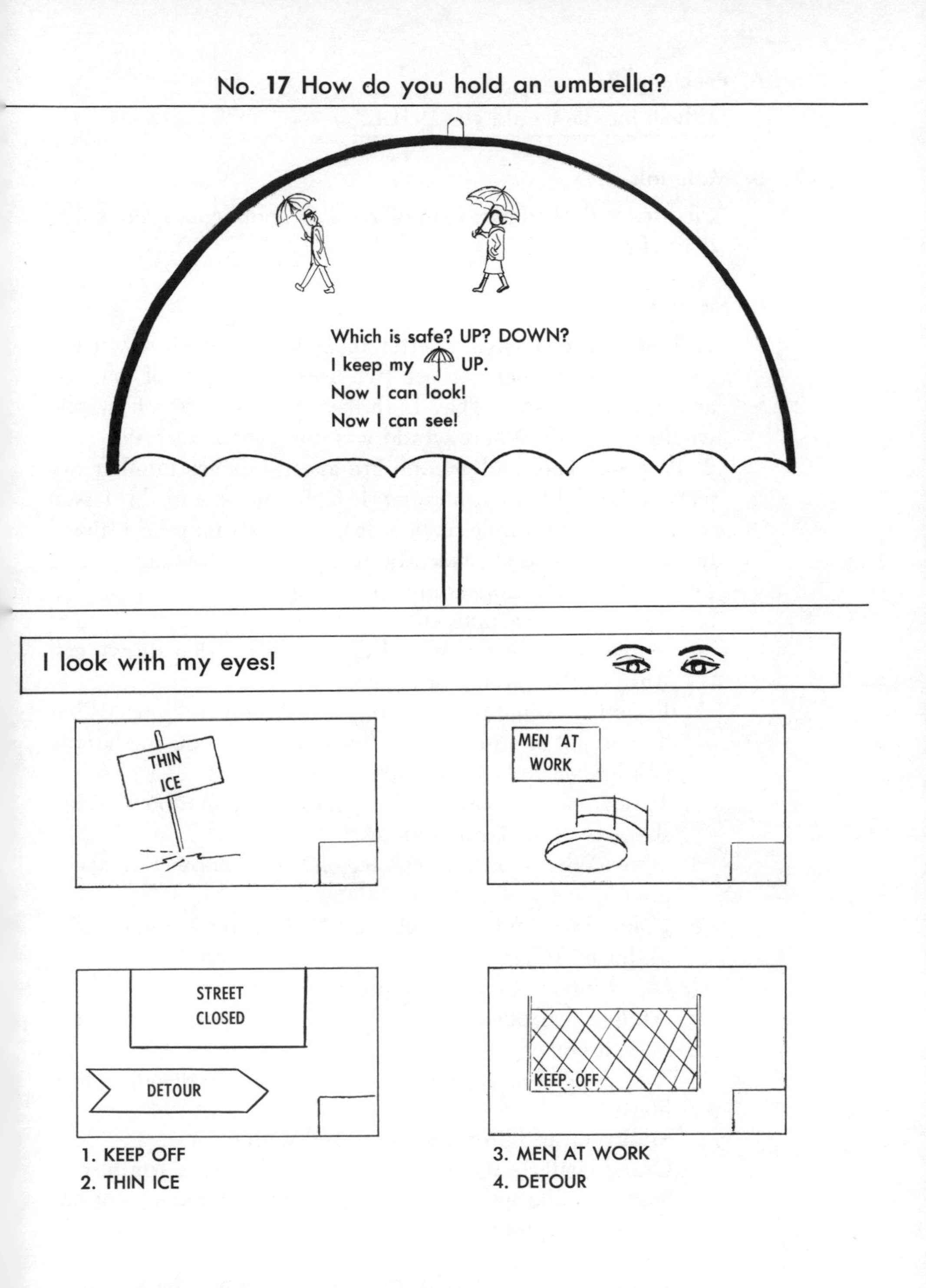

A. Problem 18

Which handle would you PULL?

B. Materials

Pictures and word cards: mailbox, P.O., mailman, firebox, fire dept., fireman

C. Method

1. Teacher: You have a letter to mail. You walk down the street. At the corner you see two boxes (pictures of mailbox and fire alarm box). They both have handles. Which handle would you pull? Where would you put your letter? Why?
2. Purpose: The mailbox and fire alarm box are familiar objects in the child's environment. It is the purpose of this lesson to provide an example of how learning aids may be utilized to develop concrete associations. See the following section (name, function, appearance, color, signs).
3. Discussion – learning aids
   a. Name: Establish names of each object. What do we call "this"? (Use picture or object.)
   b. Function: What do they do? How do they help us? What do you put in a mailbox? Why would you pull the handle of a fire alarm box? When?
   c. Appearance – shape: What shape is a mailbox? What shape is a fire alarm box?
   d. Signs: What words do you see on the mailbox? Fire alarm box?
   e. Color: What color is each box? What color is a mailman's uniform? What color is a fireman's uniform?
   f. Other information (examples)
      "Helpers" associated with the problem (postman or mailman, fireman)
      "Building" associated with the problem (post office, firehouse)
      Mailtruck and firetruck associated with each
      Orange ball designates the location of a fire alarm box
      Some mailboxes are for the mailman's storage, not for mailing purposes.
4. Vocabulary
   a. Pictures and word cards for each: mailbox – firebox, post

office – fire dept., mailman – fireman

b. Drill: match words and pictures

c. Games (examples)
Which belong together? Sort cards.
Child picks a card. What is it? Match it.

d. Board games and drill

5. The topic may be divided into two lessons after the problem has been introduced. Concepts associated with each are taught separately.

a. Lesson 1: The mailbox, post office, and mailman

b. Lesson 2: The firebox, fire dept., and fireman

D. Solution

1. We put letters in a mailbox.
2. We use a fire alarm box to get help.
3. Our eyes help us to recognize different objects.
4. Many objects in the environment help people (to keep safe, to communicate).

E. Learning Aids and Environmental Vocabulary

1. Name: mailbox, fire alarm box
2. Function: to send letters, to keep us safe
3. Shape: box
4. Signs: U.S. MAIL, FIRE ALARM
5. Color: red, red and blue
6. Helper: mailman, fireman
7. Building: POST OFFICE, FIRE DEPT.

F. Related Problems

1. What other signs are associated with the topic MAIL? (STAMPS, LETTERS, and other post office signs.)
2. How does a fire extinguisher help us?
3. What is the purpose of a fire escape?
4. What happens to a letter after you put it in a mailbox?
5. How do you behave during FIRE DRILLS? FALLOUT SHELTER DRILLS?

G. Teacher Directions

Problem Worksheet No. 18

1. Review of each sign and concept associated with the problem
2. Picture discussion
3. Review concept and DO YOU KNOW?
   a. NAME
   b. COLOR
   c. HELPER
   d. SIGN
4. Discuss problem worksheet directions orally. Have children read aloud.
5. Direct children to follow each direction at bottom of problem worksheet.

H. Suggested Activities

1. Visits to post office and firehouse
Note: Many mentally retarded are employed at P. O.'s. Observe work duties.
2. How to turn in a fire alarm. Dangers of false alarms.
3. Mathematics: stamps, Special Delivery (cost).
4. How to address an envelope. Letter writing form.
5. Learn to read directions on each box. (See Information Sheet.)
   a. Mailbox – TIME SCHEDULE
   b. Firebox – directions

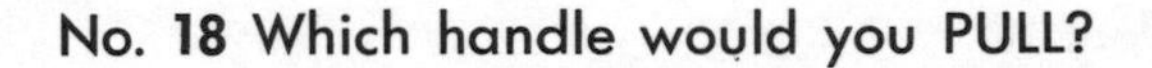

No. 18 Which handle would you PULL?

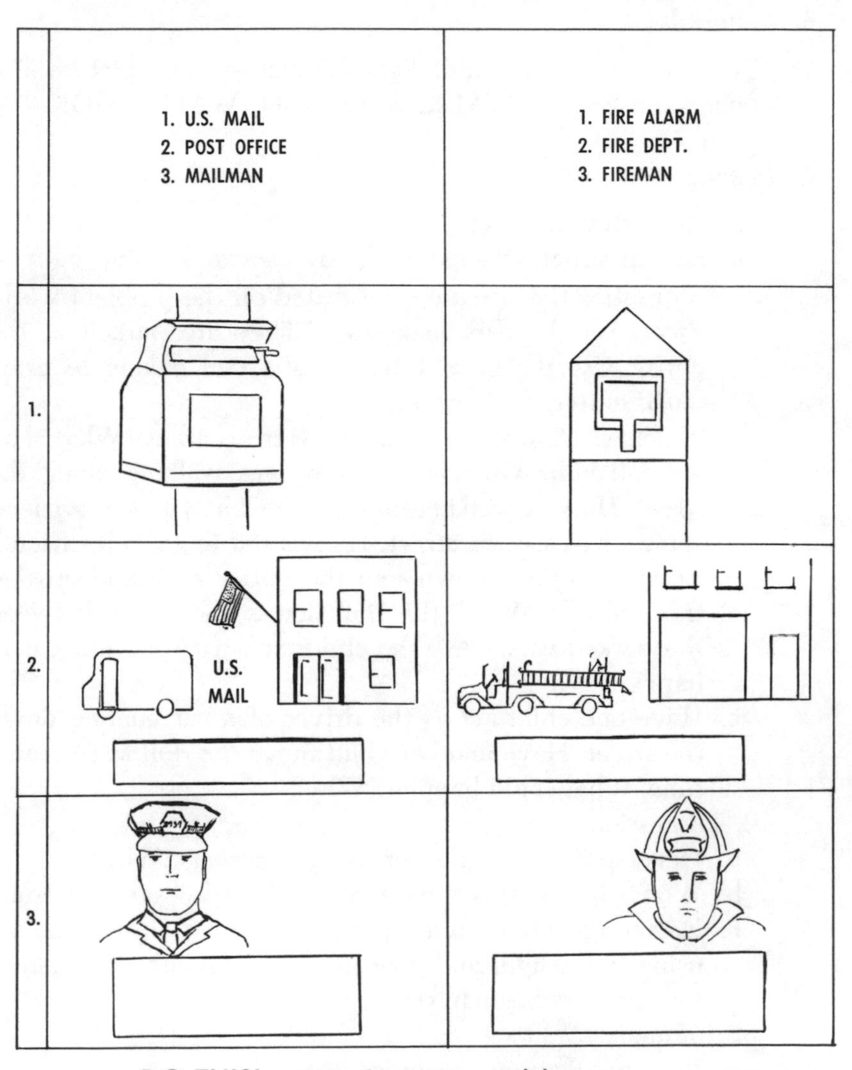

DO THIS! Write the name on each box.
Write the name of each building under the picture.
Write the name of each helper under the picture.
COLOR the pictures. (1 - 2 - 3).

A. Problem 19

How do you cross the street?

B. Materials

Toy cars, small doll, traffic light (circles or box), picture of a policeman. Signs – WALK, STOP, GO, WAIT, LOOK.

C. Method

1. Demonstration
   a. Set up situation – use doll, toy cars and traffic light to reproduce the situation illustrated on the problem worksheet. Set the cars in a row. "They are parked at the curb." Use the floor, table, or sheet of oaktag to draw curb, gutter, and corner.
   b. Teacher: (Show doll to class.) Here is a boy. What shall we call him? One day Tommy was walking along the street. He was walking on the sidewalk. He saw a friend standing across the street. He wanted to go to his friend. Tommy stepped down into the gutter here and crossed the street. ("Walk" the doll across the street between the parked cars.) Ask the children what they think may happen. Why?
   c. Have one child act as the driver of a car coming down the street. Have another child move the doll at the same time. What could happen? Why?
2. Discussion
   a. Develop the concept of crossing at corners. Why?
   b. Who helps us cross at corners? (Policeman, safety patrol.)
   c. Encourage children to participate in a dramatization, using traffic light and policeman. (Turn light to green or red. Have policeman signal.)
3. Summary
   a. Review rules and concepts.
   b. Develop rules from demonstration. What do we do if . . . ?
   c. How do signs, lights and the policeman help us?

D. Solution

1. Cross at the corner where you can be seen.

2. When you cross between parked cars, the car coming down the street cannot see you.
3. Cross when the light is green.
4. Look for signals from the policeman.

E. Learning Aids and Environmental Vocabulary

1. Colors
   a. Red – STOP, DANGER. Green – GO. Yellow – WAIT or CAUTION
   c. Policeman's uniform – blue
   b. Policeman's gloves – white
2. Signs – STOP, GO, WAIT, WALK, DO NOT WALK
3. Signals – Traffic light, policeman's hand signals, car directional signals

F. Related Problems

1. What other signals help to keep us safe in the street? (Car directional signals, WALK, DO NOT WALK, etc.)
2. What color clothing is easily seen at night?
3. Why does the policeman wear white gloves?
4. How would you cross the street if there were no traffic light or helper?
5. How does a push-button traffic light work?

G. Teacher Directions

Problem Worksheet No. 19

1. Read story chart on the problem worksheet.
2. Dramatize each sentence.
3. Review signs and colors.
   a. Red means danger.
   b. Traffic light: red on top, yellow in middle, green on bottom
   c. STOP – GO – WAIT – LOOK
4. Policeman
   a. His work – how he helps us
   b. How he signals. His hands tell you what to do.
   c. How do you know he is a policeman? Uniform (blue), badge (POLICE DEPT.), whistle, etc.
5. Problem Diagram

a. Direct children to put an X on the figure of the child who is crossing at a dangerous place.
b. Direct children to put a circle around the child who is crossing at the corner.
c. Color the light to mean that the child may cross the street safely. Color the policeman's uniform.

6. "When I Cross"
a. Finish each rule. Review orally. (Refer to story chart.)
b. Fill in a word, or color a picture for each: 1 – STOP or red circle. 2 – LOOK or blue circle. 3 – WAIT or yellow circle. 4 – GO or green circle.

H. Suggested Activities

1. Discuss: how we cooperate with the police dept. (Rules, regulations and safety patrol helpers.)
2. Signals: Cars use blinkers, directionals and horns. Bicycles use lights and bells. What hand signals do you use when you ride a bicycle?
3. How does a traffic light work? Demonstration – use flashlight and colored papers.
4. Write and draw illustrations of safety signs.
5. Additional safety lessons
a. How do push-button lights work?
b. What should you do when your ball rolls into the street?
c. Discuss other helpers who keep us safe.

No. 19 How do you cross the street?

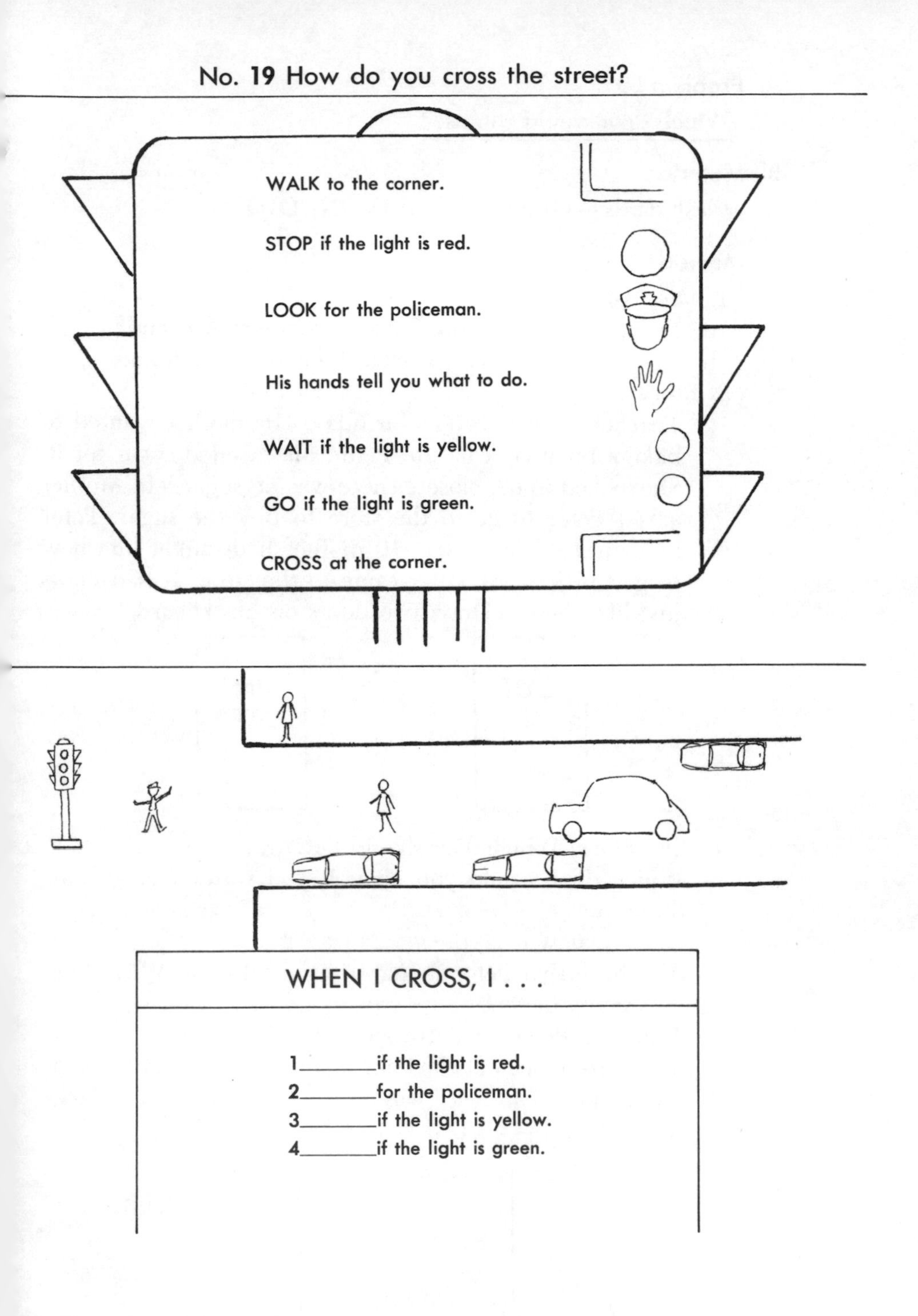

A. **Problem 20**

Which door would you use?

B. **Materials**

Flash cards – OPEN, CLOSED, IN, OUT

C. **Method**

1. Discussion
   a. Do you go to the store for your mother? A friend?
   b. Encourage children to relate their own experiences.
2. Story
   a. Teacher: It was Peter's birthday. His mother wanted to bake a birthday cake for Peter. She needed sugar for it. She looked in her closet. There was no sugar left. Mother asked Peter to go to the store to buy the sugar. Peter knew just where to go. His mother had taught him how to go to the store. Peter came to the store. It had doors just like these. (Draw two doors on blackboard.)

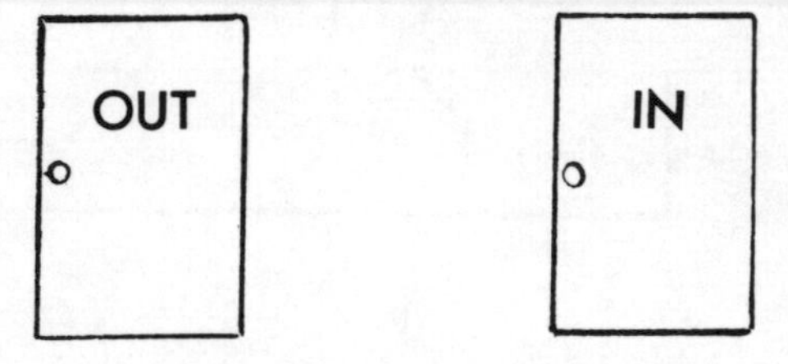

   b. Questions: Which door should Peter use?
      Which door would you open if you wanted to go into the store?
      Do you know what the words "say"?
      (Establish that Peter should use the IN door. Why? Discuss safety factors.)
   c. Teacher: Peter tried to open the door, but it did not move. He looked at the door again. He saw another sign on the door. This word was on it. (Draw a door on blackboard. Word – CLOSED.)

d. Questions: Do you think Peter could go into the store? Why?
(Establish that store is CLOSED.)
How did Peter feel?
What should Peter do?
What would you do?

e. Teacher: Peter leaves. Peter came back to the store a little later. There was a new sign on the door. (Draw a door on the blackboard. Word – OPEN.)

f. Questions: Could Peter go into the store now? Why? How did Peter feel?

g. Teacher: Peter bought the sugar. He had a happy birthday after all!

D. Solution

1. Signs help us. They tell us what to do.
2. We use the IN door to enter a store or building.
3. We use the OUT door to leave a store or building.
4. When a sign reads OPEN, we can go into a store or building.
5. When a sign reads CLOSED, we cannot go into a store or building.

E. Learning Aids and Environmental Vocabulary

1. Signs
2. IN
3. OUT
4. OPEN
5. CLOSED

F. Related Problems

1. Why do you use a lock?
2. How do you use a key?
3. How do you use a doorknob?
4. What other signs are related to the topic? (EXIT, ENTRANCE, OPEN, COME IN, etc.)

G. Teacher Directions

Problem Worksheet No. 20

1. Review each sign with the class.
2. Use blackboard and flash cards for drill exercises. (Exam-

ple: Invite a child to find the word that tells you the store is open.)

a. Match cards and words on blackboard.

b. Invite children to write words on the blackboard.

3. Instruct children to color the box (under the door) Green for the sign that reads IN. Color the box Red for the sign that reads OUT. Color the box Blue for the sign that reads OPEN. Color the box Yellow for the sign that reads CLOSED. Teacher should prepare this as a blackboard exercise before the children complete the assignments on worksheets.

4. Note: The teacher who uses this problem worksheet with an individual child, for survey or diagnostic purposes may instruct the child to mark X or a sign in the correct box.

5. Have the children write the appropriate sign on each door on the problem worksheet. Teacher should prepare this as a blackboard exercise before the children complete the assignment on worksheets. Example:

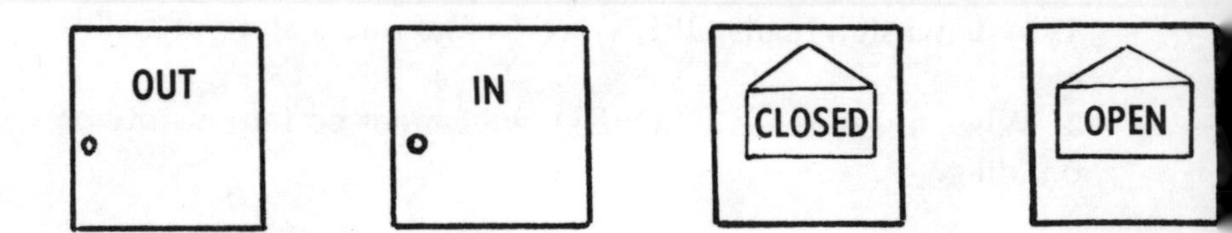

H. Suggested Activities

1. Discuss and formulate safety and directional rules for using doors marked IN, OUT, OPEN, CLOSED, ENTRANCE, EXIT.

2. Relate to mathematics.

   a. STORE HOURS – clock example – OUT TO LUNCH, WILL RETURN AT 2 O'CLOCK

   b. Days – Open Monday and Thursday until 9

3. Hang or place signs on classroom door.

4. School project – construct signs for other places in the school building.

No. **20** Which door would you use?

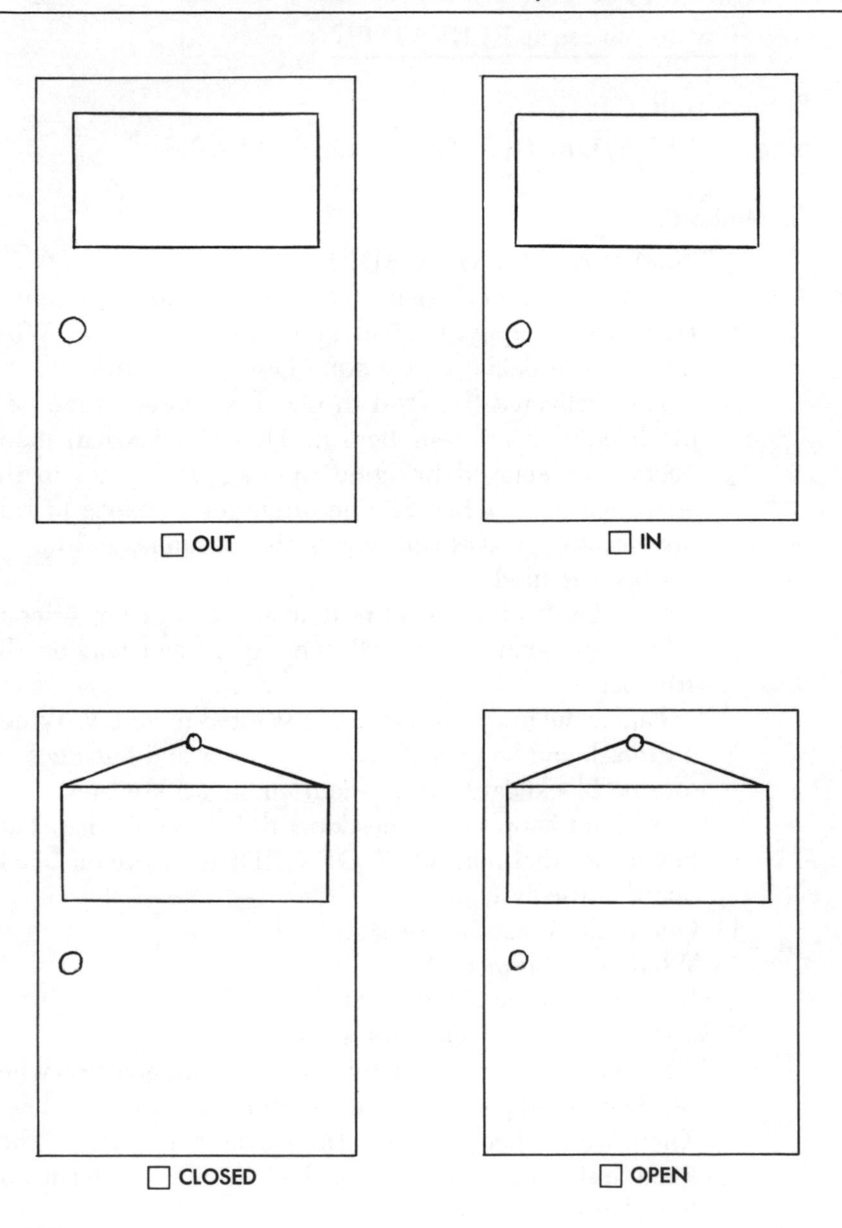

A. Problem 21

How do you use an ELEVATOR?

B. Materials

Signs: ELEVATOR, OUT OF ORDER, ALARM

C. Method

1. Situation A: OUT OF ORDER
   a. Teacher: Paul worked in a supermarket near his house. He was very happy. He had a job as a delivery boy. What work does a delivery boy do? (Discuss job duties.)

   Paul delivered the food to people's houses. Some people lived in apartment houses. These houses had many floors. Paul enjoyed bringing the bags and boxes to the apartment houses because he often got a chance to ride the elevators. It was fun to ride the elevators, and he did not become tired.

   One day Paul was told to deliver a box of groceries to a house he knew very well. The apartment was on the 4th floor.

   Paul came to the elevator. He wanted to go UP. Which button should he press? (Draw elevator and outside buttons on blackboard or use diagram on worksheet.)

   Nothing happened. The doors didn't open! Then Paul saw a sign that read OUT OF ORDER (write on blackboard or use flash card).

   b. Questions: What did the sign say?
   What does this mean?
   What should Paul do? (USE STAIRS)
2. Situation B: If the elevator stops
   a. Teacher: Another time Paul was inside an elevator when suddenly it stopped moving. It did not go up or down. There were other people in the elevator with Paul. They knew just what to do. If Paul had been alone, he would have known what to do.

   b. Questions: What would you do?
   How would you get help?
   Who could fix the elevator?

   c. Concept: ALARM
   We could call for HELP. We could push the button

marked ALARM. How does this button help? (The sound will attract other people who will hear the sound and bring help to take us out of the elevator.)

3. Discussions
   a. Guide children in a discussion of rules to follow in using the elevator.
   b. Behavior in an elevator. Stress politeness. No pushing, move to the back to make room for others, giving elevator man the floor number.
   c. Emphasize that the elevator is a way of traveling in a building. It is dangerous to play with mechanisms.
   d. Discuss the danger of holding or forcing elevator doors to open.

D. Solution

1. We observe and read signs that instruct us how to use an elevator.
2. Buttons and switches help us to use the elevator safely.
3. We follow safety rules.
4. Elevators take us from floor to floor quickly.

E. Learning Aids and Environmental Vocabulary

1. Signs: ELEVATOR, OUT OF ORDER, ALARM
2. Directionals: UP ↑ DOWN ↓
3. Color: ALARM button – red

F. Related Problems

1. How do you use elevators in public buildings and department stores? (SERVICE, FREIGHT or EMPLOYEES ONLY, EXPRESS ELEVATOR, SELF-SERVICE)
2. How do you use escalators? (ESCALATOR, UP, DOWN)
3. How do you use revolving doors? (PUSH HERE, PUSH SLOWLY)
4. Should you hang around (loiter) on stairs and hallways?

G. Teacher Directions

Problem Worksheet No. 21

1. Story: Teacher or individual child may read story to class. Story can be utilized as the basis for a reading lesson.
2. Develop procedure for using an elevator. Dramatization.

(Push button UP or DOWN, push button for FLOOR No. 4.)

3. Review signs and labels.

4. Complete "FLOOR No.?" exercise on problem worksheet.
   a. Discuss purpose and function of FLOOR No. "clock." How does it work? (Pointer)
   b. Instruct children to draw the correct pointer that will match the number or word written under each clock. Example: Demonstrate.

5. Buttons and signs
   a. Discuss purpose and functions of each.
   b. Read each sign and label.
   c. Instruct children to match the words in the column with the buttons. Draw a line.
   d. Which button would you press to open doors? Close doors? STOP the elevator?, etc.

6. Note: This problem may be divided into several lessons according to class attention span and ability level.

H. Suggested Activities

1. Story: Read, write or illustrate according to academic level.
2. Make a list of all the signs you find in the story.
3. Dramatize situations (see Related Problems).
4. Children inform class about other elevator signs and buttons. Example: LOBBY, FIRST FLOOR (in their apartment houses).
5. Colors: What color is the alarm or emergency switch? What colors are used to designate DOWN or UP? What color is associated with danger? (Red) Construct a booklet of colors – where they are seen, and how they are used in the community. Examples: traffic lights, flashing blue and amber lights, train lights, etc.

No. 21 How do you use an ELEVATOR?

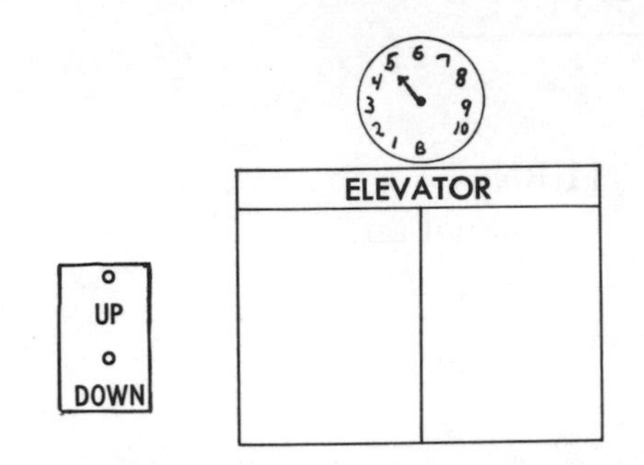

I like to ride in an ELEVATOR. The ELEVATOR is fast! I can go from the FIRST FLOOR to the top. It is faster than the STAIRS. I push the button when I want to go UP or DOWN. I know what to do in the ELEVATOR. I push the button that takes me to my floor. Sometimes the ELEVATOR is OUT OF ORDER. I know what the signs mean. I know what the buttons mean. Do you?

FLOOR NO. ?

7

BASEMENT

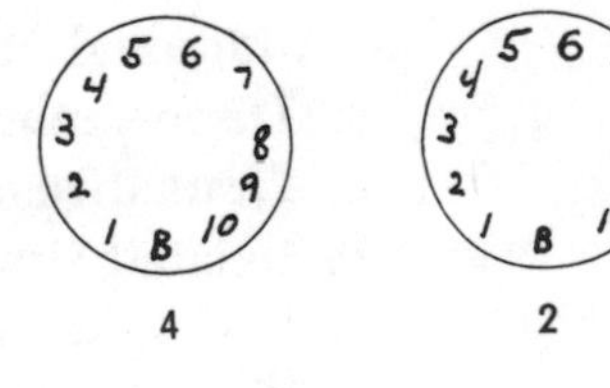

4

2

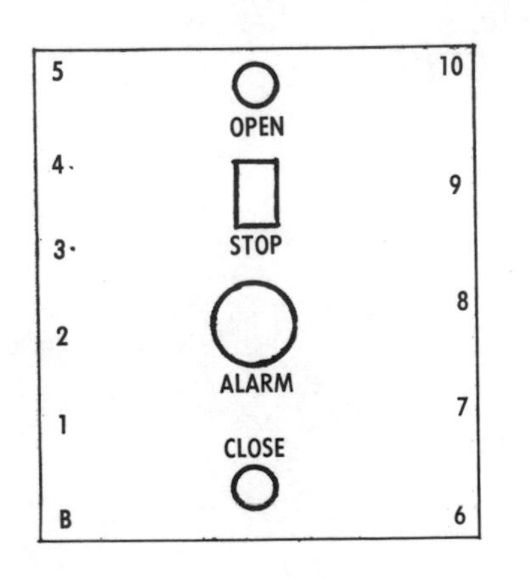

OPEN
STOP
FLOOR No. 4
CLOSE
BASEMENT
ALARM

A. Problem 22

Would you PUSH, TURN, or PULL?

B. Materials

Word cards: PUSH, PULL, TURN
Pictures related to problem – see situations.

C. Method

1. Discussion
   a. How our hands help us
   b. How our fingers help us
   c. What can you make each do?
2. Demonstration
   a. Develop situations outlined on problem worksheet. Use as a guide.
   b. Use pictures, blackboard diagrams, or concrete objects to develop each. Example: Here is a tube of TOOTH-PASTE. How do you open it? TURN.
   c. Demonstrate how we use our fingers and hands in each situation. Encourage children's participation in demonstrations. Note position of hand and fingers when we PUSH, PULL or TURN.
3. Additional situations
   a. Discuss other situations which involve each concept.
   b. Dramatize other situations.
   c. Related situations: revolving or "accordion" doors, mailbox, light switch, towel machines, water faucets, jar tops, dials on radios and clocks, etc.
   d. Do you PUSH, TURN or PULL?
      How do you use each?
      What signs help you?
4. Summarize
   a. How do you PUSH?
   b. How do you PULL?
   c. How do you TURN?
   d. When would you do each?
   e. Where do you see these signs?

D. Solution

1. Our hands and fingers help us to do many different things. (Function)
2. We use our hands to PUSH revolving and swinging doors, turnstiles and other objects.
3. We use our hands and fingers to PULL window shades, mailboxes, and other machines.
4. We use our fingers to TURN jar covers, dials, water faucets and other objects we use daily.

E. Learning Aids and Environmental Vocabulary

1. PUSH
2. PULL
3. TURN
4. Signs explain how to use objects that are in the environment

F. Related Problems

1. What safety factors are involved in using objects and machines? (Turnstile, revolving door, etc.)
2. How do you use clocks, TV, radio and other objects that have dials?
3. What should you know about hand care? (Wash, nail brush, etc.)
4. How can we learn to develop muscles and finger dexterity?

G. Teacher Directions

Problem Worksheet No. 22

1. Discuss each story situation on the problem worksheet.
2. Read each story aloud.
3. Dramatize each situation.
4. Review
   a. Concepts
   b. Signs
5. Instruct children to write signs in space on door, tube, machine.
6. "What Would You Do?"

a. Review orally.
b. Children check correct column. Add other examples.

H. Additional Activities

1. Riddles: What would you do? Relate to PUSH, PULL, TURN concepts. Add other concepts: PRESS, LIFT, etc.
2. Provide experiences to develop dexterity. Health Education activities: balls, ring toss, etc. Arts and Crafts activities: metalwork, sewing projects, etc.
3. Construct a classroom chart. Duplicate the worksheet page. Add other examples of situations related to PUSH, PULL, TURN.
4. Discuss and develop safety rules related to problem. Example: how we use a swinging door, CANDY – MILK – ICE machines, and turnstiles safely. Stress manners, waiting turn, caution, etc.

No. 22 Would you PUSH, TURN, or PULL?

You have 2 hands.
You have 10 fingers.
You use them in many ways!
PUSH — TURN — PULL

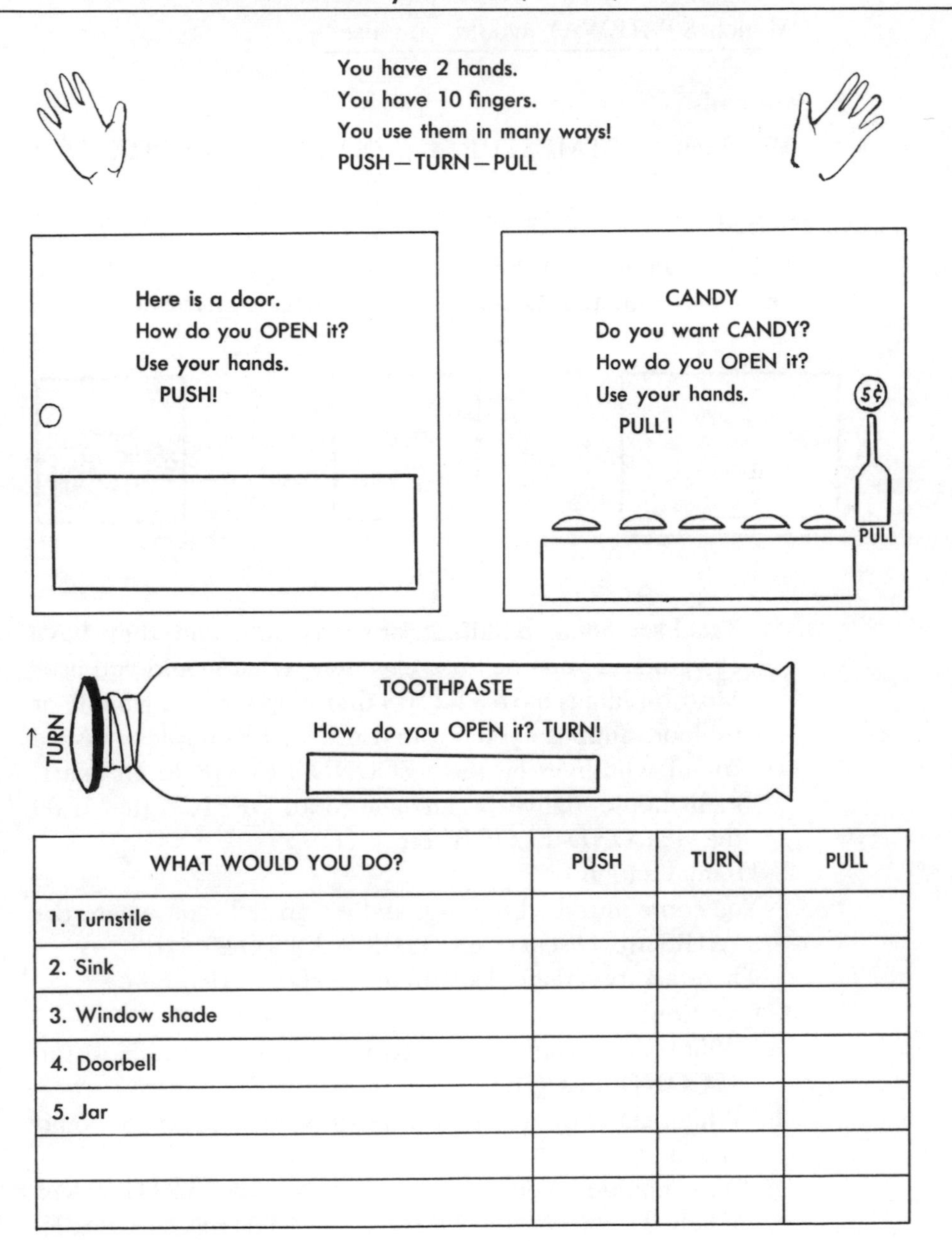

WHAT WOULD YOU DO?	PUSH	TURN	PULL
1. Turnstile			
2. Sink			
3. Window shade			
4. Doorbell			
5. Jar			

A. **Problem 23**

Which STAIRWAY would you use?

B. **Materials**

Word cards: STAIRS, UP ↑ , DOWN ↓ , FLOOR

C. **Method**

1. Situation A: STAIRS
   a. Draw sign and 2 doors on blackboard as pictured below:

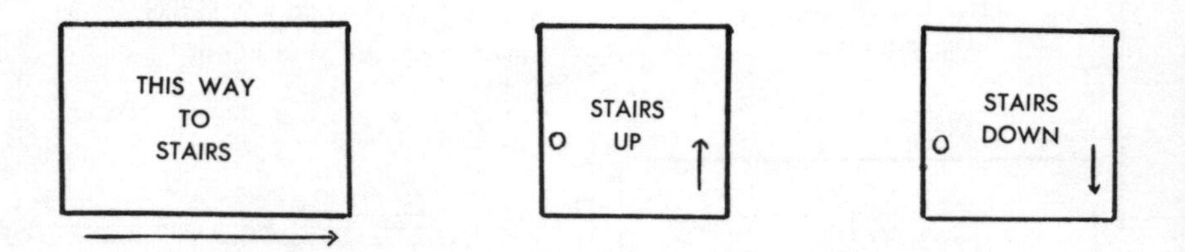

   b. Teacher: Some buildings are very tall, and they have elevators. If you don't use elevators, what would you use? Most buildings have STAIRS that help you get from floor to floor. Suppose you wanted to . . . (Examples: Visit a friend who lives on the SECOND FLOOR in an apartment house, deliver a package to an OFFICE that is on the SECOND FLOOR, etc.)
2. Dramatization
   You come into the building, and a sign tells you where the STAIRS are. Discuss sign, THIS WAY TO STAIRS →
   There are two doors like these. (Refer to diagram.)
3. Questions
   a. Which door would you open to go (get) upstairs to the SECOND FLOOR?
   b. Which stairway would you need? Which STAIRS would you use?
   c. Why couldn't you use the DOWN ↓ STAIRWAY? When do you use the DOWN ↓ STAIRWAY? BASEMENT?
4. Use word cards. Review.
5. Situation B: FLOORS
   Teacher: Suppose you want to go (get) to your friend's

apartment (or an OFFICE). It is on the SECOND (next) FLOOR.

6. Questions
   a. Is there a sign that tells you that you are on the SECOND FLOOR?
   b. Have you ever seen such a sign?
   c. What else could there be? (Number) (Use word sign — FLOOR.)
7. Concepts — discuss
   a. UP ↑ — FIRST, SECOND, THIRD
   b. DOWN ↓ — BASEMENT: Which STAIRS would you use to get to the BASEMENT?
8. Note: Each situation can be the basis for two separate lessons.
   a. STAIRS
   b. FLOORS

D. Solution

1. We use STAIRS to go from FLOOR to FLOOR in buildings.
2. We use the UP ↑ STAIRS to climb to the next floor or floors above.
3. We use the DOWN ↓ STAIRS to get to the floor or floors below.
4. Signs and arrows tell us how to get there and where we are. Examples: UP ↑ , DOWN ↓ , FLOOR 2, FIRST FLOOR

E. Learning Aids and Environmental Vocabulary

1. Signs: STAIRS, UP ↑ , DOWN ↓ , FLOOR
2. Concepts: FIRST, SECOND or Nos.; BASEMENT ↓ , TOP ↑
3. Arrows → , ↑ , ↓ point the way.

F. Related Problems

1. What does EXIT mean when it is written above the sign STAIRS or STAIRWAY? EMERGENCY EXIT?
2. How does a DIRECTORY (office or house) help you?
3. Why should you KEEP OFF roofs of buildings?
4. For what is a BASEMENT used? What do you find in a BASEMENT?

5. What safety rules should you follow when using STAIRS?

G. Teacher Directions

Problem Worksheet No. 23

1. Review and drill words related to problem.
2. Direct children's attention to diagram at top of problem worksheet (Situation A).
   a. Discuss Situation A.
   b. Follow the X's. Draw a line connecting X's.
   c. Begin at the left.
3. Signs – develop situation.
   a. You come into a building – IN (door).
   b. THIS WAY TO STAIRS →
   c. STAIRS ↑ UP, SECOND FLOOR.
   d. Example: Deliver package to OFFICE.
   e. STAIRS ↓ DOWN
   f. You leave the building – THIS WAY OUT →
4. Direct children's attention to two buildings. (Situation B)
   b. Discuss Situation B.
   a. Concepts FIRST, SECOND, THIRD. Review 1 – 2 – 3 – 4 FLOOR Nos.
   c. Children "fill in" second building. They can use floor nos. or words: FIRST, SECOND, BASEMENT (or B).
5. What other signs do you see on doors?
   a. Row of doors
   b. Review orally. Examples: IN, OUT, OPEN, BOYS, GIRLS, OFFICE, etc.
   c. Discuss where each sign is found. What others?
   d. Direct children to write signs related to this or other problems.

H. Suggested Activities

1. List other signs related to the problem. Illustrate meanings. Charts. Examples: STAIRWAY, EXIT, LOBBY, KEEP OFF ROOF, USE STAIRS
2. Learn to read a DIRECTORY found in OFFICE buildings. Where? (LOBBY) Names of people, companies, floor numbers.
3. Learn to read information related to a house: name, apartment number, floor number.

4. Safety rules — review
   a. How to walk up and down STAIRS
   b. How to carry packages up and down STAIRS
   c. School rules for using STAIRS and EXITS

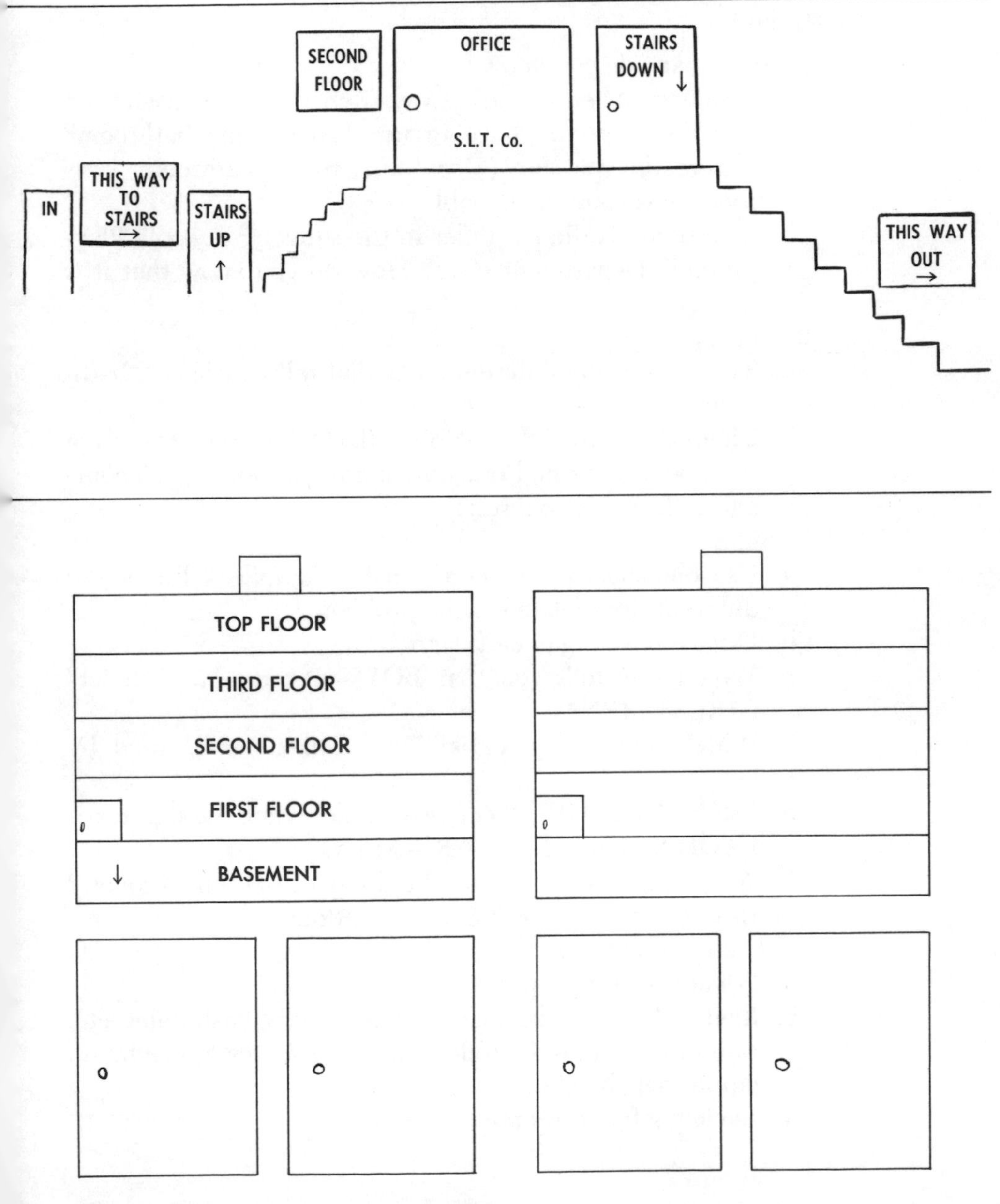

A. Problem 24

Which TOILET would you use?

B. Materials

Word cards: TOILET, BOYS, GIRLS, MEN, WOMEN, etc.

C. Method

1. How many do you know?
   a. Teacher: When you are away from your house, what do you do when you have to use (go to) the bathroom? Where do you go? (Use terms toilet, bathroom, restroom, etc., interchangeably.)
   b. Questions: Is there a toilet in the subway? School? Playground? Department store? How do you know that it is a toilet?
2. Survey:
   a. There are many different signs that tell us where a bathroom is.
   b. There are many different signs that tell us who can use a bathroom. Let's find out how many you know. (Encourage children's responses.)
3. Signs
   a. Use blackboard and word cards. Compile a list of the different signs related to the problem.
   b. Discuss meaning of each sign.
   c. Which sign tells you that BOYS may use "this" toilet? GIRLS? MEN?
   d. Which signs tell you that "this" toilet can be used by both?
   e. Establish that GIRLS can use a toilet when the sign reads LADIES. Similarly, BOYS – MEN.
   f. What signs do you see on the doors of the school toilets? In department stores? Service stations?
4. Related discussions
   a. Privacy – using separate booths
   b. Review hygienic practices – wash hands, flush toilet, etc.
   c. Equipment in public toilets: pay toilets, towel machines, liquid soap, hand dryers, etc.
   d. Review safety rules related to topic.

D. Solution

1. Different words that help us know where to find a toilet (bathroom) when we are away from our homes.
2. The signs tell you who can use a toilet – BOYS, GIRLS.
3. We should read signs on doors very carefully.

E. Learning Aids and Environmental Vocabulary

1. BOYS – GIRLS
2. MEN – WOMEN
3. TOILET – RESTROOM – BATHROOM

F. Related Problems

1. Should you linger ("hang around") in public toilets?
2. How can you help keep our public toilets clean?
3. Do you use other people's bathrooms carefully?
4. Why should you close the water faucet after washing your hands?

G. Teacher Directions

Problem Worksheet No. 24

1. Discuss directions orally.
2. Picture discussion:
   a. Boy (Man)
   b. Girl (Woman)
   c. Man and Woman
3. Review each sign.
4. Instruct children to read each sign carefully. Draw a line from the sign "to the one who may use the toilet or bathroom." Note that some signs are appropriate for both sexes. Emphasize that these toilets are used at different times (for privacy).
5. Explain that signs are often written in other languages – for example, Spanish.
6. Copy signs. Write in space at bottom of sheet.

H. Suggested Activities

1. Instruct children to keep a list of signs related to topic and "where I saw it" (school, neighborhood stores). Examples: PAY TOILETS, TOWELS, HOT or COLD WATER, FLUSH TOILET

2. Food unit: Discuss proper diet associated with keeping healthy. (Example: roughage foods)
3. Stress the importance of keeping bathrooms clean. Use of detergents and disinfectants. Discuss hazards. Signs and labels on boxes and cans: POISON, etc.
4. Develop appreciation of workers who clean and repair toilets, restrooms, bathrooms: plumbers, park and office helpers who clean public toilets. Study work duties, and tools used. Observe these people at work. Invite speakers to class.

No. 24 Which TOILET would you use?

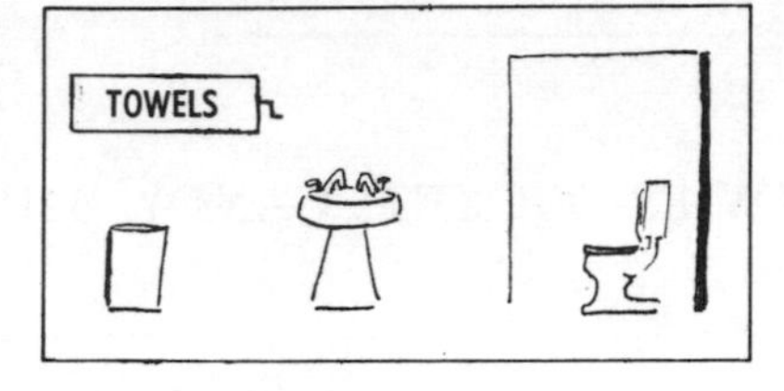

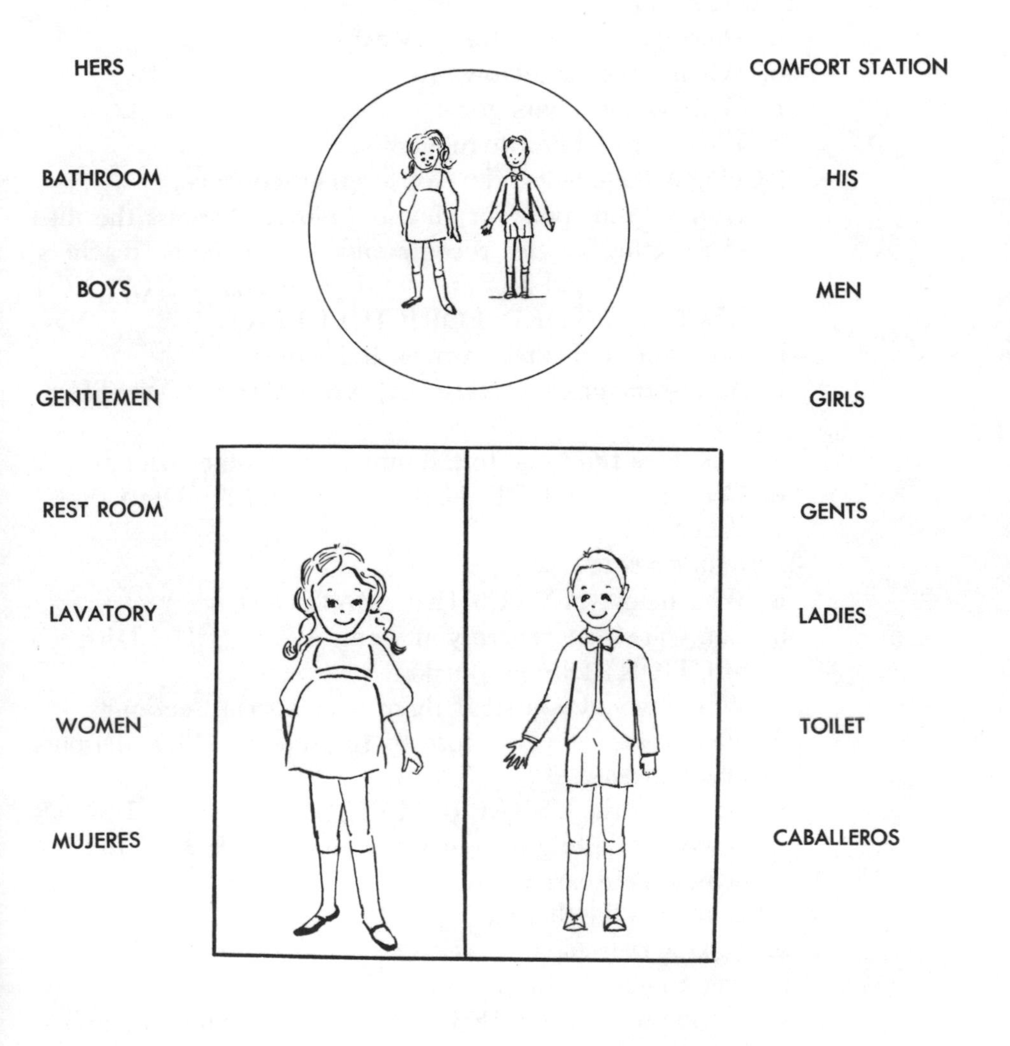

A. Problem 25

What do you do at the MOVIES?

B. Materials

Signs: MOVIES, TICKET, CANDY, THE END

C. Method

1. Discussion
   a. Do you like to go to the movies?
   b. When do you go? How often?
   c. With whom do you go?
   d. What is your favorite movie?
2. Going to the movies: develop steps in sequence.
   a. How do you "pick" or choose a movie? Discuss the idea of selecting movies recommended by parents, teachers, and recreational leaders (FOR ADULTS ONLY, NOT RECOMMENDED FOR CHILDREN).
   b. Location of theater (travel and money)
   c. Admission price (CHILDREN'S ADMISSION, TICKET)
   d. It is more fun to go to the movies with other friends.
   e. Getting a TICKET (Use sign.) How? (Dramatize.) Why?
3. Finding a seat
   a. Who helps you? (USHER, MATRON)
   b. Can you sit anywhere you want? Why? (CHILDREN'S SECTION) Discuss purpose.
   c. Where would you sit if there is no special section?
   d. Should you sit very close to the screen? Why? Discuss effect on eyes.
   e. How does the USHER or MATRON help you? (USHER – uses his flashlight to help you in the dark. MATRON – helps to take care of you.)
4. Behavior in the theater
   a. Talking to friends
   b. Loitering in the bathroom
   c. Staying too late (THE END). Go home when the movie is over.

D. Solution

1. Signs help to keep us safe. (CHILDREN'S SECTION)
2. People help to keep us safe. (USHER, MATRON)
3. We should learn to protect our eyes.
4. If you wear glasses, use them at the movies, when you read, watch TV, etc.

E. Learning Aids and Environmental Vocabulary

1. Movie lists
2. Signs: MOVIES, TICKET, etc.
3. Meaning of FOR ADULTS ONLY and NOT RECOMMENDED FOR CHILDREN

F. Related Problems

1. What other recreational facilities are there near your home?
2. What hazards do we associate with the park, playground, and beach?
3. How can you learn to keep busy?
4. Are you spending too much time at the movies? Watching TV?

G. Teacher Directions

Problem Worksheet No. 25

1. Teacher may read story (on problem worksheet) to class or children may take turns reading aloud.
2. Review the signs (MOVIES, TICKET, etc.).
3. Direct children's attention to the space under the story. "How many signs can you find in the story?" Have children write signs in the space or draw a picture that describes the different signs.
4. "Do you have fun? YES – NO"
   a. Discuss different ways of having fun.
   b. If a child is able to, he may answer each question by putting an X in the YES or NO column. He may write the word if he wishes.
   c. If children cannot read the question, the teacher can conduct the survey orally with the group.

H. Suggested Activities

1. Learn to read movie listings in newspapers and other guides.
2. Mathematics: cost of ticket, candy, other expenses related to attending movies. Budgeting an allowance for recreation.
3. Become acquainted with other signs related to the topic: FOR ADULTS ONLY, COMING ATTRACTIONS, etc.
4. Discuss other recreational facilities available: clubs, parks, museums, etc. Encourage attendance. Discuss use of, behavior at . . .
5. Encourage "listening" activities – radio, phonograph. Develop use of leisure time – hobbies, collections, handcrafts, etc. Provide experience.

No. 25 What do you do at the MOVIES?

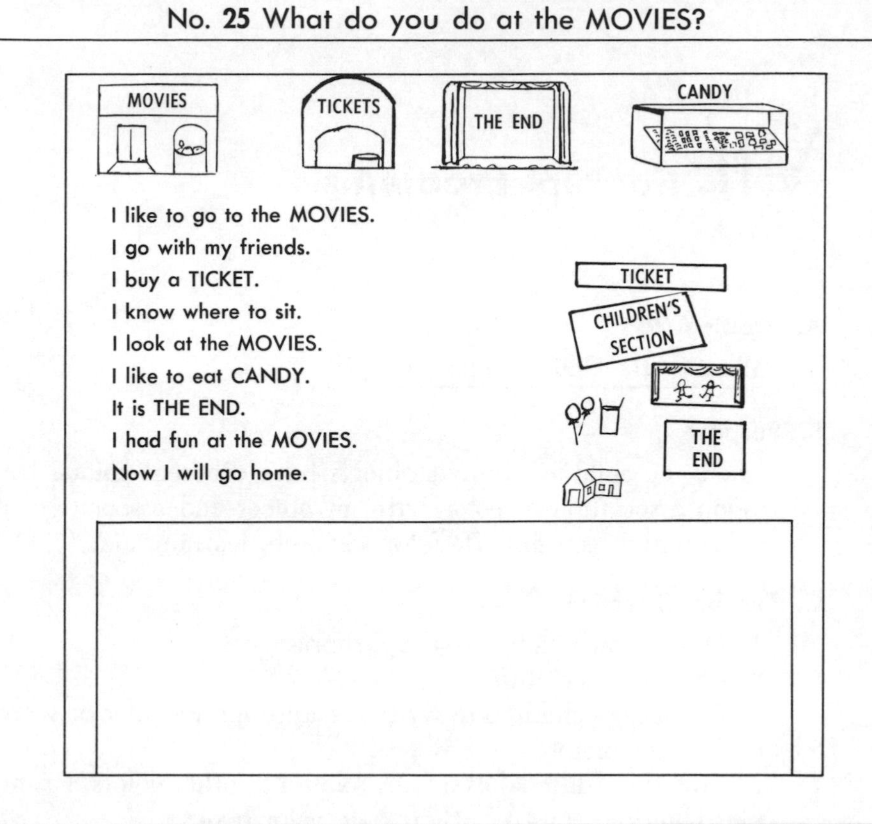

I like to go to the MOVIES.
I go with my friends.
I buy a TICKET.
I know where to sit.
I look at the MOVIES.
I like to eat CANDY.
It is THE END.
I had fun at the MOVIES.
Now I will go home.

DO YOU HAVE FUN?	YES	NO
1. I look at TV.		
2. I play with my friends.		
3. I read books.		
4. I like to dance.		
5. I go to the park.		
6. I like to make things.		
7. I listen to the radio.		
8. I like to swim.		

VII. Concept Problems

A. Problem 26

What do the COLORS mean?

B. Purpose

Make the child aware that objects have different colors. Develop association of color with an object and association of color with a concept. Develop concrete learning aids.

C. Teacher Directions

1. Discuss each picture and appropriate color.
2. Child colors picture.
3. Encourage children to write the appropriate color or word under each picture.
4. Provide additional exercises related to other colors. Example: Children construct their own color books.
5. Summarize. (Use problem worksheet.)
   a. How do colors help to keep us safe?
   b. What color uniform does each worker wear?
   c. What colors do we associate with different objects in our environment?
   d. What colors do we associate with seasons or holidays?
6. Recognition of color
   a. Names of each
   b. Word for each
   c. Learn to read each color name.
   d. Learn to write each color name.
7. Additional experiences
   a. Paints. Examples: Mix colors, experiments involving colors and shades.
   b. Crayon and chalk activities. Examples: Coloring on cardboard, newspaper, cloth, etc.
   c. Importance of color in daily living. Examples: Clothes we wear, home decoration, etc.

No. 26 What do the COLORS mean?

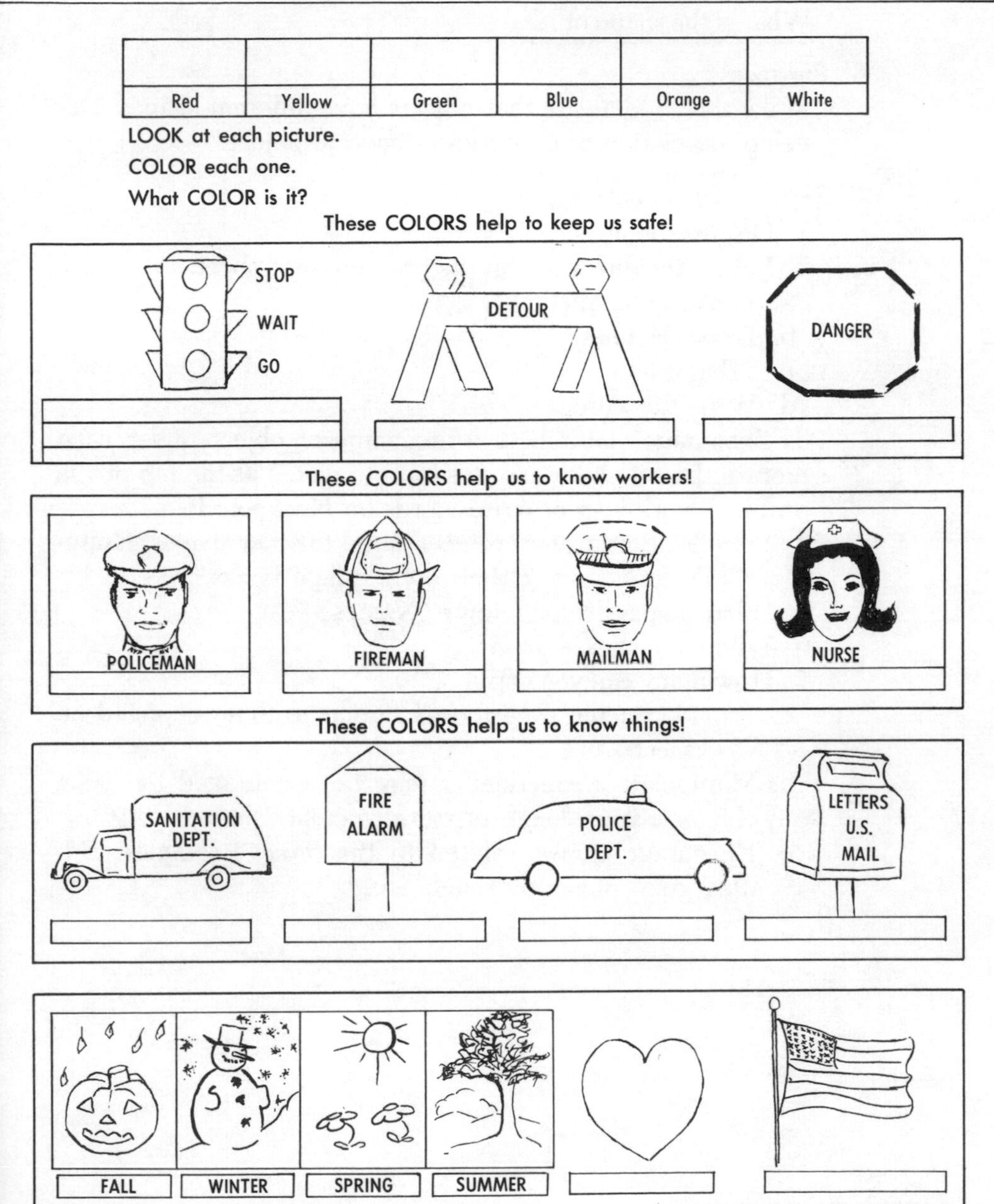

A. **Problem 27**

What is the shape of it?

B. **Purpose**

Make the child aware that objects have different shapes. Develop association of shape and concrete object.

C. **Teacher Directions**

1. Discuss shapes.
2. Follow the directions on the problem worksheet.
   a. Look at each picture.
   b. Draw the lines.
   c. What is it?
   d. Write the words.
3. Encourage children to write name of object under each picture. Direct children's attention to words at the top of the problem worksheet or write words on blackboard.
4. Provide additional exercises related to other shapes. Example: Children construct their own "shape books."
5. What shapes do you know? (Names)
6. Where do you see them?
7. How many can you copy?
   a. Provide tracing experiences similar to those depicted on worksheets.
   b. Manipulative experiences may be encouraged by using clay or a flour dough mixture to create shapes.
   c. Encourage games, related to the topic. Examples: riddles, guess object by touch, etc.

No. 27 What is the shape of it?

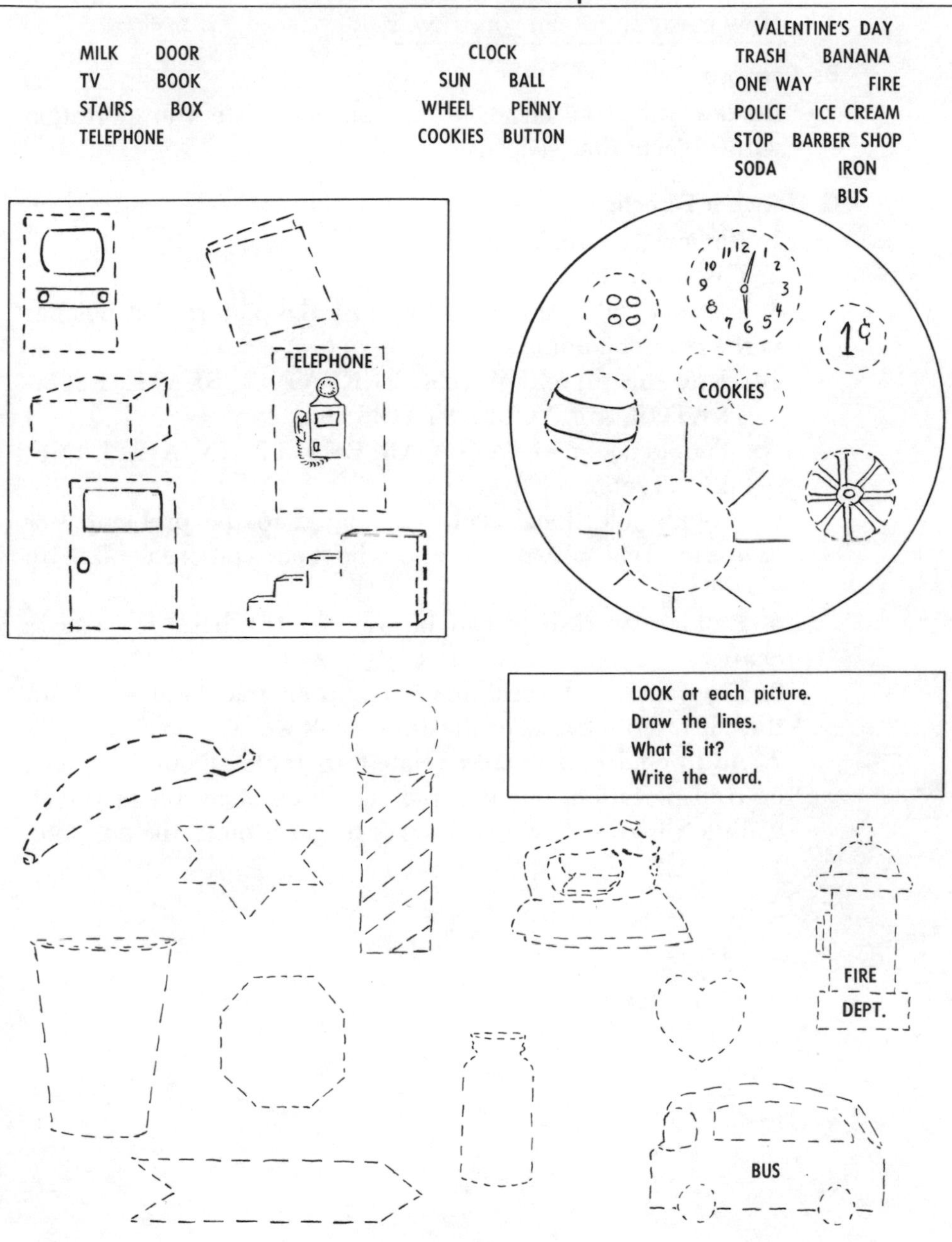

A. **Problem 28**

<u>How many ways can you travel?</u>

B. **Purpose**

Review different means of travel. Associate transportation with objects that help us.

C. **Teacher Directions**

1. Review each means of travel.
2. Discuss pictures.
3. Instruct children to write or draw the picture that belongs in the correct column.
   a. I do this myself! WALK, ELEVATOR, SKATE, ESCALATOR, BICYCLE, STAIRS, etc.
   b. People take me! TAXI, CAR, BUS, TRAIN, AIRPLANE, BOAT, etc.
4. Provide additional exercises related to the problem. For example: Who are the people who take you from place to place?
5. Problem worksheet can be used as the basis for a class chart.
6. Environmental vocabulary: Children may add words to their list, write cards, or illustrate each word.
7. Additional experiences related to topic. Examples: unit on transportation, mural depicting different means of travel, walk to discover how many ways to get around the city, etc.

No. 28 How many ways can you travel?

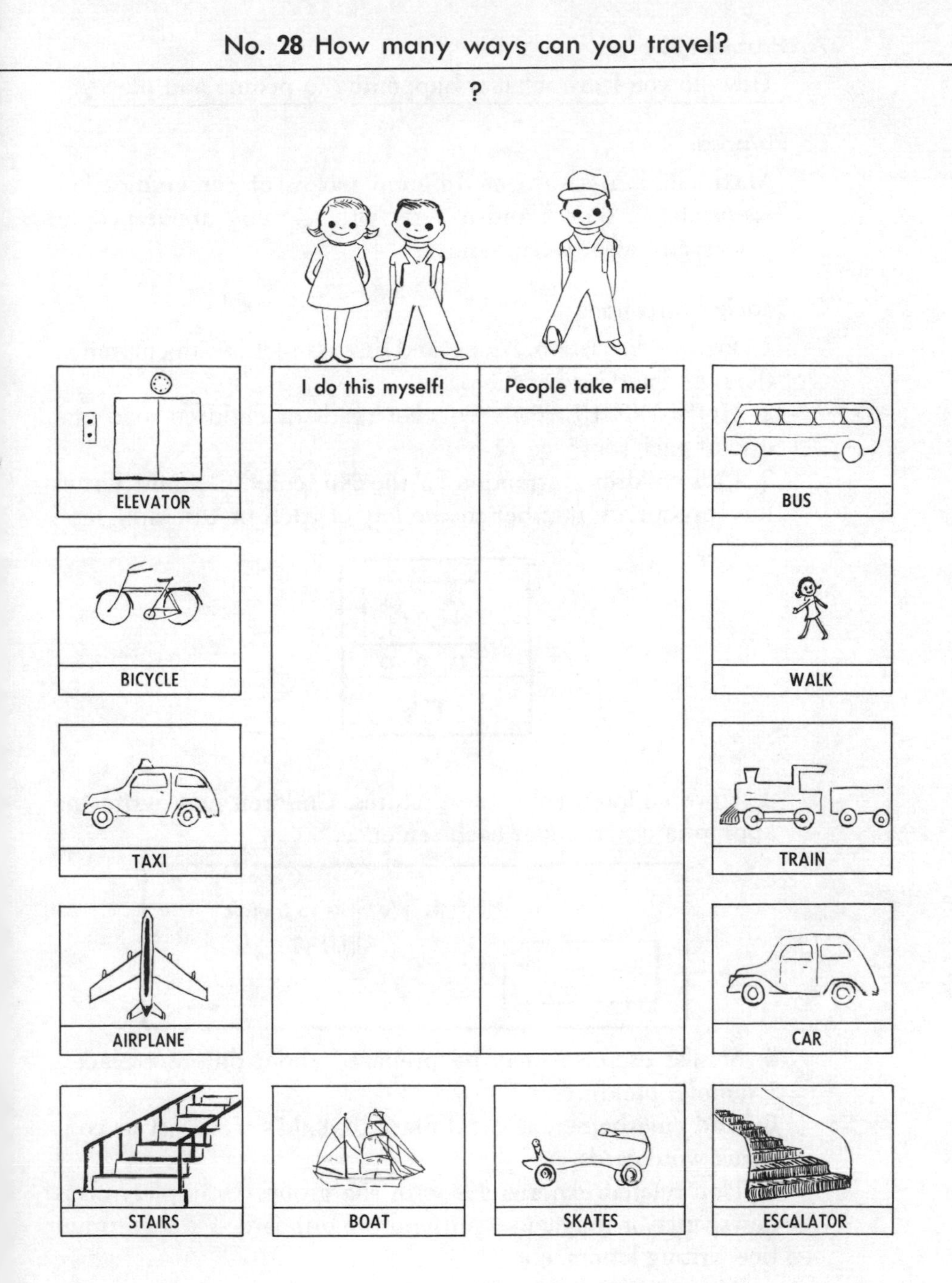

A. Problem 29

How do you learn what is happening to people and places?

B. Purpose

Make children aware of different means of communication. Associate an object and a sign with learning about people, places, and what is happening.

C. Teacher Directions

1. Picture discussion. Name and discuss pictures in column at the right hand side of the page.
2. HOW WE LEARN: Teacher reads or children read and discuss each sentence (1-8).
3. Call children's attention to the No. column. Child writes the appropriate number to the left of each picture and sign.

4. Have children color the pictures. Children may write the appropriate sign under each sentence.

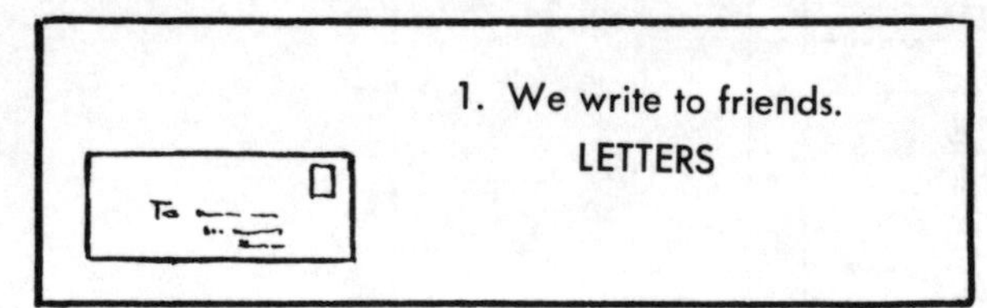

5. Similar exercises may be prepared about different places. Example: buildings.
6. Add environmental vocabulary to child's word list or construct word cards.
7. Plan related experiences with the group. Examples: class newspaper or magazine, miniature cardboard TV sets, practice writing letters, etc.

No. 29 How do you learn what is happening to people and places?

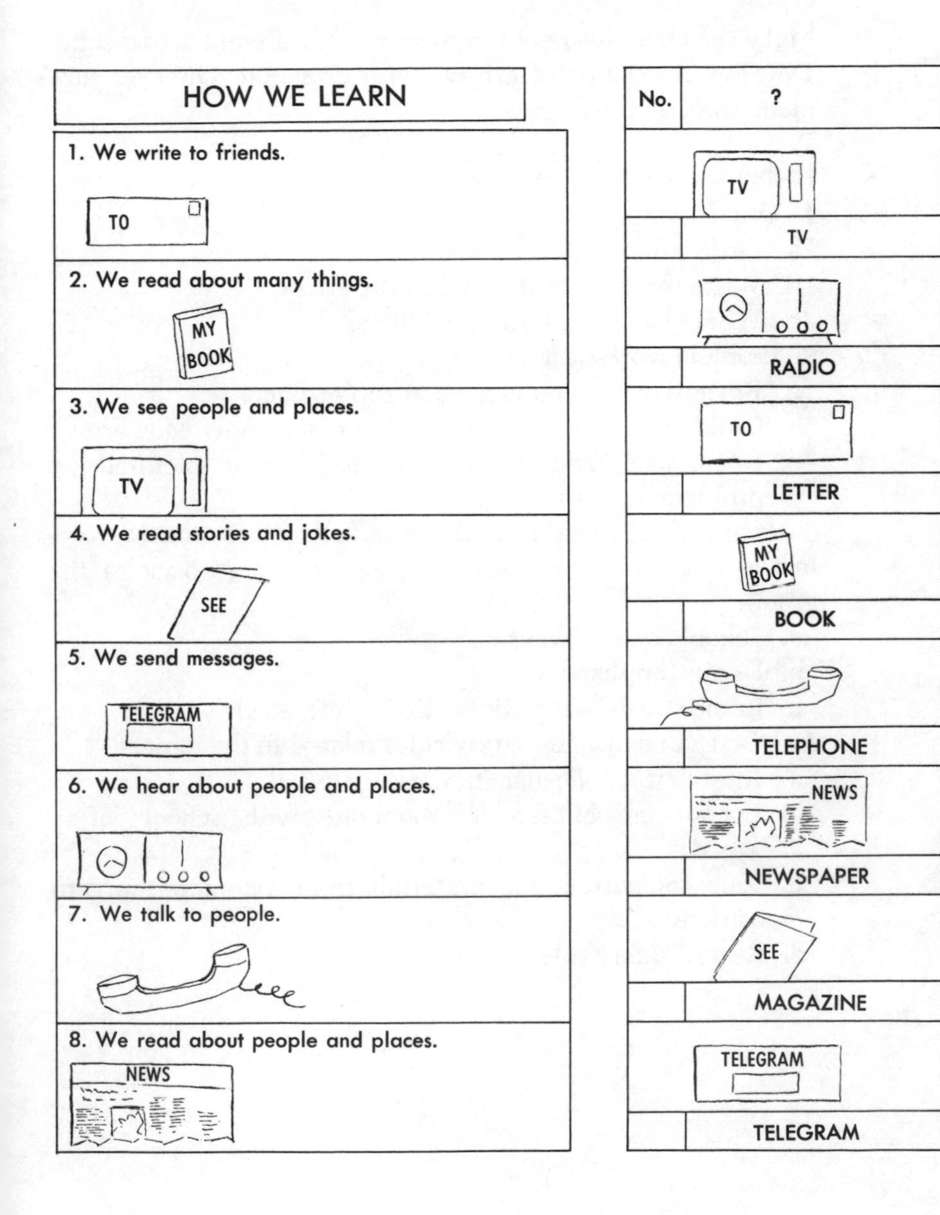

HOW WE LEARN
1. We write to friends.
2. We read about many things.
3. We see people and places.
4. We read stories and jokes.
5. We send messages.
6. We hear about people and places.
7. We talk to people.
8. We read about people and places.

No.	?
	TV
	RADIO
	LETTER
	BOOK
	TELEPHONE
	NEWSPAPER
	MAGAZINE
	TELEGRAM

A. Problem 30

<u>What do the arrows tell you to do?</u>

B. Purpose

Make the child aware of the meaning of different arrow signs. Develop association of arrows with direction. Discover how many the group recognizes.

C. Teacher Directions

1. Oral survey
   a. Draw arrows on blackboard.
   b. Write the word that matches the arrow.
   c. Where have you seen these signs?
2. Problem worksheet
   a. Review words and arrows at top of page.
   b. Child writes appropriate word in space under each arrow.
   c. Encourage children to draw each arrow pictured on problem worksheet.
3. Assign children to locate these and other directional arrows in the community. Encourage them to report back to the group.
   a. School (on stairways)
   b. Home (appliances)
   c. In the street (Keep Right, Keep Left, etc.)
4. Discuss and develop safety rules related to the topic.
   a. Interview a policeman or crossing guard.
   b. Encourage children to cooperate with school safety squad.
   c. Send for posters and materials from automobile organizations.
   d. Record safety rules.

No. 30 What do the arrows tell you to do?

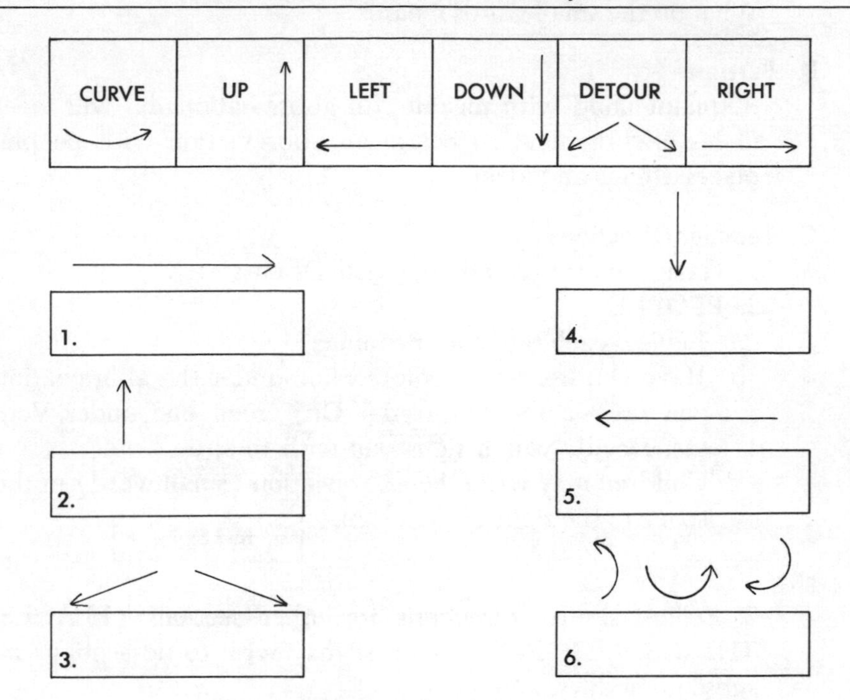

Where have you seen these?

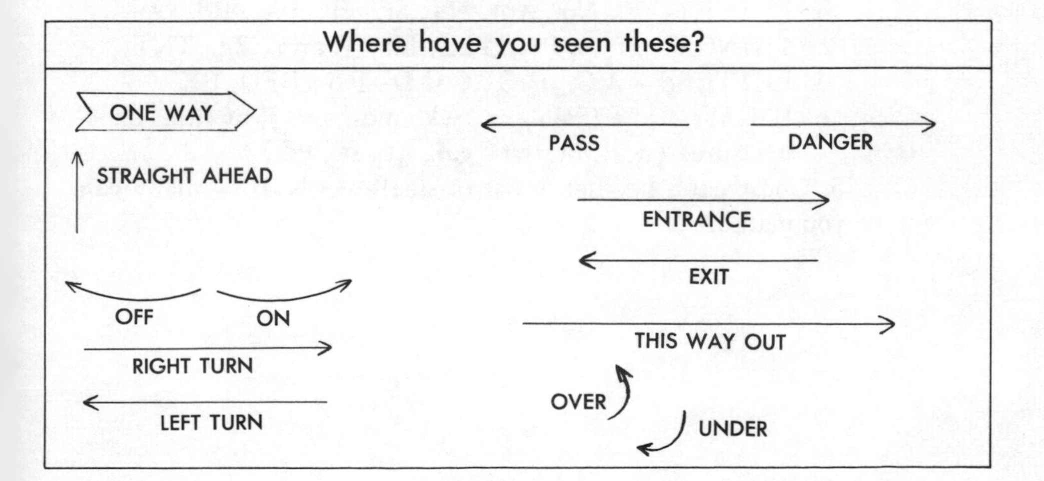

A. Problem 31

What do the small words mean?

B. Purpose

Acquaint child with meaningful abbreviations he will meet in his environment. Associate an abbreviation with people, places, things and ideas.

C. Teacher Directions

1. Have you ever seen these signs? Discuss each.
2. PEOPLE
   a. Review each sign and meaning.
   b. Have children put a colored line under the abbreviation you say – a red line under Dr., green line under Vet., etc. Decide which signs you wish to stress.
   c. Children may write the abbreviation (small word) in the space to the right of each sign.

Mr. Smith

3. Follow similar directions for other sections (PLACES, THINGS, LETTERS). Teacher may wish to do sections on subsequent days.
4. Other environmental abbreviations
   a. PEOPLE – R.N., Mad., Sec'y.
   b. PLACES – Fl. No., Apt. No., St., Pl., Ave., Rd.
   c. THINGS – Med., P.C., Pkg., Bk., Therm., Bg., TNT
   d. LETTERS – A.C., D.C., C.O.D., P.S., RFD, RX
   e. IDEAS – time (min., hr., wk., mos., etc.), months, days, measures (doz., ht., wt., gal., qt., ft., yd.)
5. Construct a booklet or list of small words. How many can you match?

No. 31 What do the small words mean?

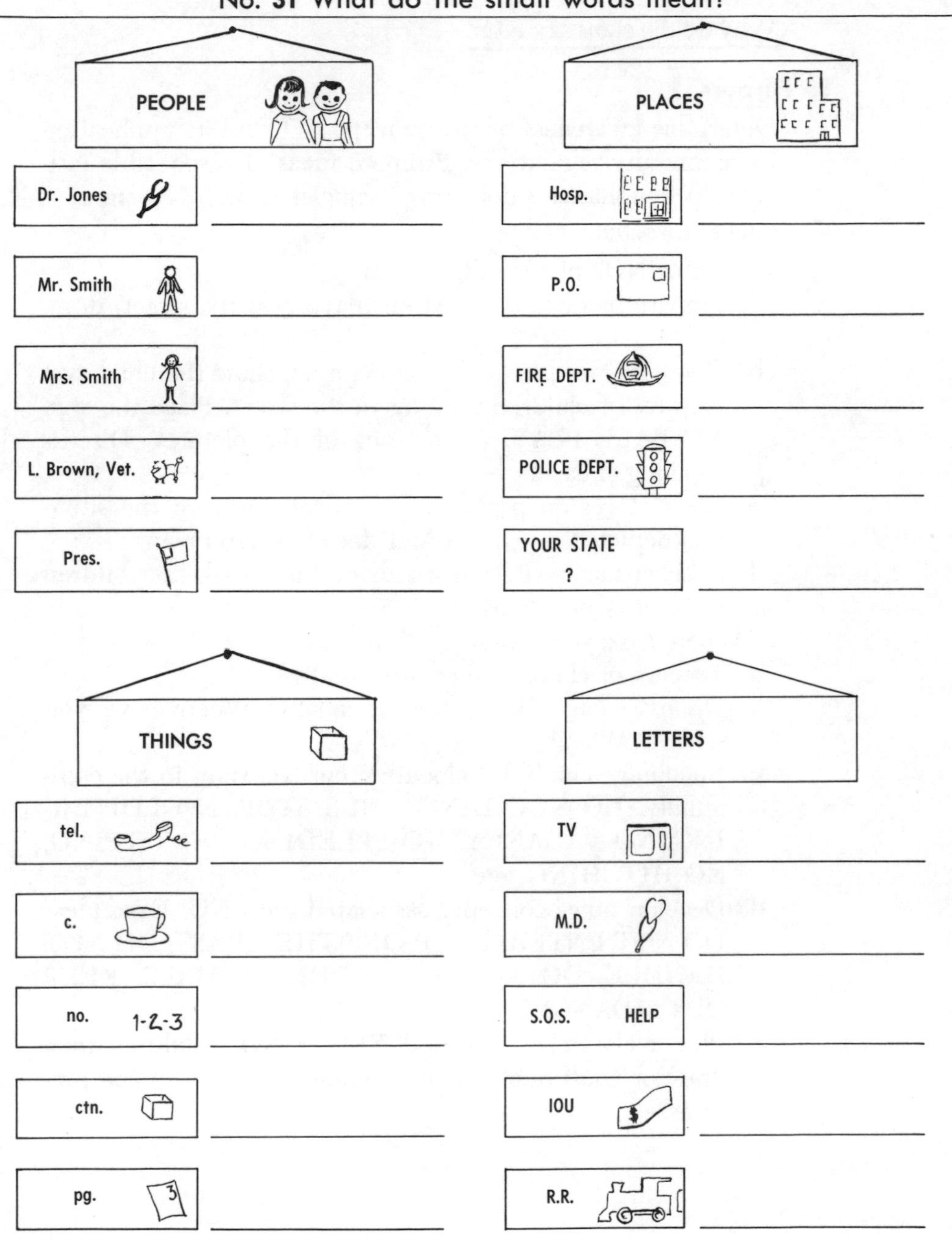

A. **Problem 32**

Why do the signs say NO?

B. **Purpose**

Determine awareness of the concept NO, and its application to community regulations. Promote ideas of responsible citizenship. Emphasize safety rules associated with NO signs.

C. **Teacher Directions**

1. YES or NO? picture discussion
   a. Prepare pictures of children playing in the street, dogs, cars, trucks.
   b. Compare two pictures. For example, show the child two pictures of children playing in the street. Place the sign NO BALL PLAYING on one of the pictures. Discuss meaning of each.
   c. See pictures on problem worksheet. Develop the situation depicted in each. What does the sign mean?
   d. Teacher may write the words on the board, ask children to identify or underline.
2. Where have you seen it?
   a. Teacher or children read list (orally).
   b. Discuss each – What does it means? Where have you seen it? When?
   c. Encourage children to locate other NO signs in the community. NO STANDING – BUS STOP, NO LOITERING, NO VACANCY, NO SPEEDING, NO TIPPING, NO HITCHING, etc.
   d. Develop other concepts associated with NO. Examples: DO NOT ENTER, KEEP OFF THE GRASS, DO NOT HANDLE, DO NOT FEED THE ANIMALS, KEEP OUT – DANGER.
   e. Plan a class chart entitled YES or NO? Children may draw or contribute pictures, match words with the pictures, etc.

No. 32 Why do the signs say NO?

YES or NO?

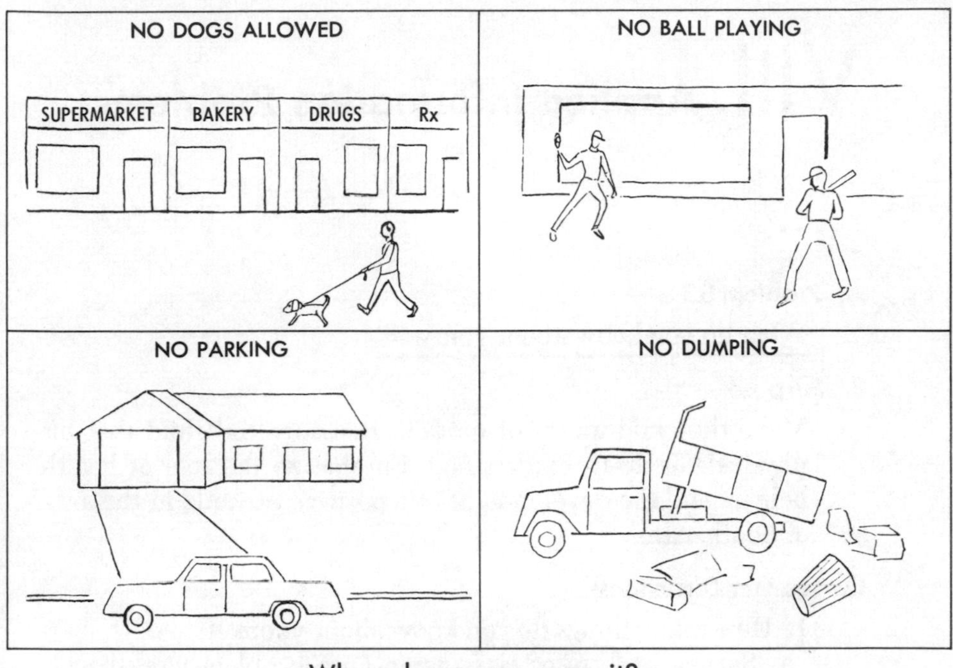

Where have you seen it?

1. NO SKATING TODAY
2. NO TURNS
3. NO BICYCLE RIDING
4. NO TRESPASSING
5. NO SWIMMING
6. NO FISHING
7. NO TALKING
8. NO SMOKING
9. NO VACANCY
10. NO STANDING

VIII. Applied Information Problems

A. Problem 33

What do you know about yourself?

B. Purpose

Make the child aware of himself. Reassure the child that his physical needs are understood. Emphasize the role of health helpers and the development of a positive attitude in the area of bodily care.

C. Teacher Directions

1. How many things do you know about yourself?
   a. Survey in form of class game (use problem worksheet).
   b. Assist children in filling in information on sheet.
   c. Provide review for those children who need further help.
2. Discussion – DO YOU KNOW?
   a. Stress a positive approach and aim to reduce fears (examples: vaccinations, doctors).
   b. Discuss community facilities: hospitals, clinics, etc.
   c. Stress signs: HOSPITAL, AMBULANCE, DR., etc.
3. Why should we know this information?
   a. Relate to forms and questionnaires required in hospitals, clinics, when applying for a job, etc.
   b. What other information should you know?
   c. How can we cooperate with our health helpers?
4. Writing experiences
   a. Provide further review of each item. Examples: Name, Age, etc.
   b. Stress importance of writing carefully and clearly.
   c. How many signs can you write? HOSPITAL, TELEPHONE, NURSE, etc.

No. 33 What do you know about yourself?

Name ______

Address ______

Date of Birth ______ Age ______

Ht. ______ Wt. ______ Sex — Male ______ Female ______

Color of Hair ______ Color of Eyes ______

Your Doctor's Name ______

Hospital ______ Health Clinic ______

Your Dentist's Name ______

Dental Clinic ______

DO YOU KNOW?

1. Why do you get shots? Vaccinations?
2. Who gives them to you?
3. What is the name of the HOSPITAL nearest your house? CLINIC?
4. What do you call the DOCTOR who takes care of your eyes?
5. What is a FIRST AID STATION?
6. How do you dial the TELEPHONE when you need an AMBULANCE?

A. **Problem 34**

What should you know about yourself in an EMERGENCY?

B. **Purpose**

Make the child aware of the importance of personal data to be used in emergency situations.

C. **Teacher Directions**

1. The teacher should fill in or assist child in completing biographical information on sheet.
2. It is also the teacher's responsibility to provide review of this information.
3. Situations should be related to environmental problems that the child encounters (if a child is lost, police inquiries, future job applications, etc.).
4. Discuss the Do You Know? questions in the problem worksheet. Read and review each question with the child.
5. Become acquainted with other forms.
6. Related situations
   a. When you are alone in the house
   b. Medicines and poisons
   c. Using the telephone in an EMERGENCY
7. Other experiences
   a. Read a variety of forms.
   b. Practice filling in information required on school forms.
   c. Signs: SCHOOL NURSE, MEDICAL OFFICE, POLICE STATION, CUSTODIAN, etc.
   d. Construct a class book of forms and questionnaires that children have seen or used.

No. 34 What should you know about yourself in an EMERGENCY?

Name ______________________________

Address ______________________________

City ______________ State ____________ Zip Code ______

Pvt. House ______________________ Apt. No. __________

Tel. No. ______________________

Parent's Name ______________________________

Bus. Tel. No. ______________

In case of an EMERGENCY call ______________________

Name of person ______________________________

Address ______________________________

Tel. No. ______________________

DO YOU KNOW?

1. What is the name of a close friend or relative? ______________________
2. Where does he live? ______________________ Tel. No. ? __________
3. Who would you go to for help? ______________________
4. Do you know the names of neighborhood helpers? ______________________
5. What is the name of your school? ______________ No.? __________
6. What is the name of your teacher and principal? ______________________
7. Where is your school? ______________________ Room No.? __________

A. Problem 35

Do you know what the words tell you to do?

B. Purpose

Make the child aware of the importance of following directions. Develop the association of words, with the ability to carry out a task.

C. Teacher Directions

1. Picture discussion
   a. The fire alarm box
   b. The mailbox
2. Do you know what each sign (directions) means? How do they help us?
3. Review each orally. Read aloud. Each topic can be a separate lesson.
4. Mailbox
   a. Meaning of HOURS OF COLLECTION
   b. Meaning of DAILY
   c. Meaning of SAT., SUN., HOLIDAYS
   d. Meaning of A.M. and P.M.
5. Discussion: DO NOT TAMPER WITH BOX
6. Review: how we mail a letter
7. After discussion, have children write the TIME in appropriate column. (A.M.-P.M.)
8. Fire alarm box
   a. Read each sign.
   b. Review meaning of each sign. Stress the dangers of false alarms.
   c. Color the box. What colors are each box?
   d. Note the two types of fire alarm boxes. Where do you see them? (Left – in the street. Right – in buildings) Encourage children to copy each set of directions. Make a class chart.
9. Begin a class book of meaningful directions. Example: directions on canned foods, appliances, etc.

No. 35 Do you know what the words tell you to do?

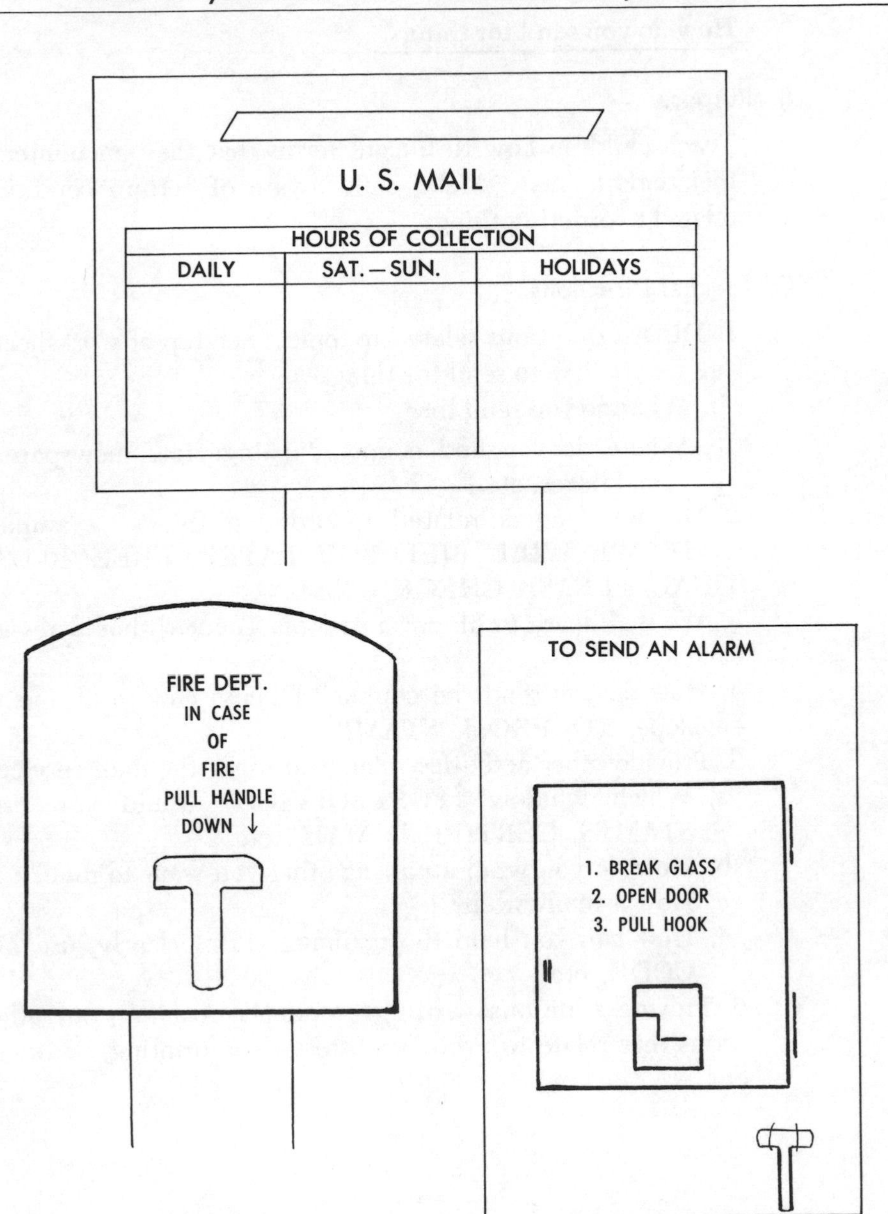

A. Problem 36

How do you send for things?

B. Purpose

Teach children how to fill out forms that they encounter in their environment. Make child aware of certain conditions related to ordering things.

C. Teacher Directions

1. Discuss questions related to topic. (See top of worksheet.)
   a. Do you like to send for things?
   b. What do you send for?
   c. Where do you find coupons? (Magazines, newspapers, cereal boxes, etc.)
2. Discuss dangers related to ordering things (examples: COST, WE WILL BILL YOU LATER, FREE 10-DAY TRIAL, PLEASE CHECK ONE).
3. We shall learn to fill out a coupon. Teacher should review each item.
4. How do you send the coupon? Discuss how to fill out an envelope. TO, FROM, STAMP.
5. Provide other activities related to using the mail service.
   a. Which window (POST OFFICE) would you use? STAMPS, CERTIFIED MAIL, etc.
   b. How do you wrap a package that you want to mail?
   c. How is mail sorted?
   d. How can you help the mailman? Print clearly, use ZIP CODE, etc.
6. Provide additional writing experience in filling out other forms that relate to problem. Stress clear printing, neatness, etc.

No. 36 How do you send for things?

Do you like to send for things?
How do you do it?
Is it FREE?
Does it cost money?
What do the words mean?

FILL IN AND MAIL TODAY

Fun Toy Co.
2318 Main Street
New York 11230

Please send me a FREE COLORING BOOK.
There is no cost.

Name ____________________

Address ____________________

City ____________ State ________

Zip Code ____________

FROM

STAMP

TO

A. Problem 37

How do you find your favorite program?

B. Purpose

Make the child aware of guides and schedules. How do they help us? Teach the child how to read a TV or radio schedule.

C. Teacher Directions

1. Discuss children's favorite programs (TV or radio). Encourage children to relate their experiences.
2. Use or provide examples of different guides that are available.
   a. TV listings in newspapers
   b. Radio listings in newspapers
   c. TV magazines (weekly)
3. Read the story chart on the worksheet. Discuss the meaning of each sentence.
4. Environmental vocabulary
   a. PROGRAM, TV, RADIO
   b. Days of week, time of day
   c. Symbols (ON-OFF, channel numbers, dials)
5. DO YOU KNOW?
   a. Read aloud with children.
   b. What information helps you to find your favorite program?
   c. Use a TV schedule for this section. Assist children to fill in questions.
6. Relate to other curriculum areas.
   a. Review days of the week, abbreviations, time symbols.
   b. Dramatize, write about a favorite show, actors, actresses.
   c. Discuss time spent, other activities and hobbies.
   d. Consider other schedules that help us: newspaper listings, bus and train schedules, store hours, etc.

No. 37 How do you find your favorite program?

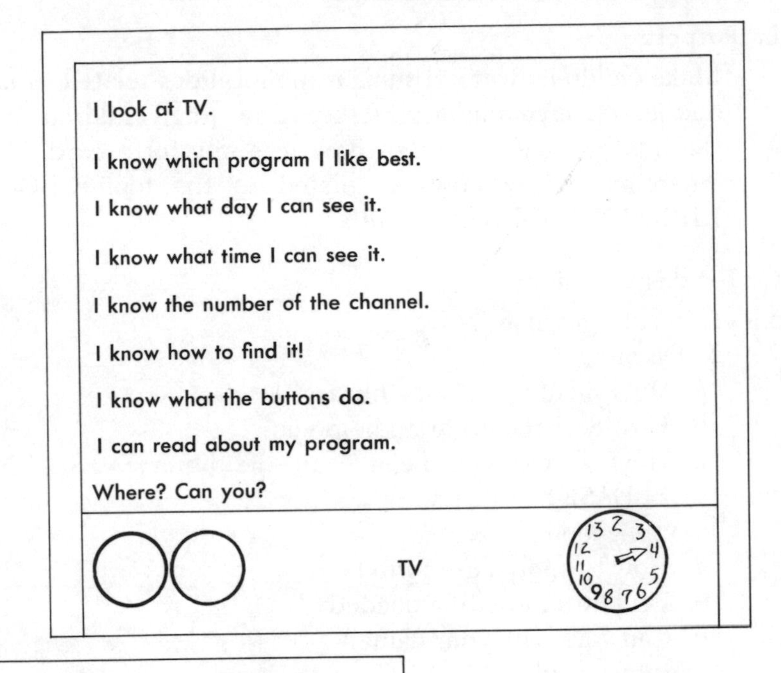

DO YOU KNOW?

1. What is the name of your favorite program?

   ____

2. On which day can you see it?

   ____

3. What time do you see it?

   ____

4. What are the names of the actors and actresses?

   ____

5. What is the program about?

   ____

A. Problem 38

How do you use the LIBRARY?

B. Purpose

Make children aware of their responsibilities related to using and joining a community facility. Encourage children to join the library. Teach children how to apply for a card. Teach environmental vocabulary related to the topic: BOOKS, LIBRARY, LIBRARIAN, etc.

C. Teacher Directions

1. Read signs aloud.
2. Discuss
   a. Why should you join a library?
   b. How does the librarian help you?
   c. How should you behave in the library? (SILENCE PLEASE)
3. Application
   a. How to apply (use form)
   b. Review information needed.
   c. Can you write your name?
4. Library card
   a. Discuss responsibility for returning books on time.
   b. Fines
   c. Care of books (keeping books clean and safe, etc.)
5. Other information
   a. Library hours
   b. Exhibits and other functions
   c. Films at the library
6. Assist child in filling out application form and library card on information worksheet.
   a. Provide additional help for those children who need it.
   b. Provide review and drill of environmental vocabulary.
   c. Set up a class library.
   d. Relate to joining other groups — community centers, Scouts, etc.

No. 38 How do you use the LIBRARY?

LIBRARY

The LIBRARY is fun!
You can take BOOKS home to read.
Sometimes you see MOVIES at the LIBRARY.
Sometimes the LIBRARIAN reads stories.
The LIBRARIAN helps you find books.
Join the LIBRARY today!

BOOKS

APPLICATION

Name ______________________

Address ______________________

Tel. No. ______________________

School ______________________

Parent's Name ______________________

LIBRARY CARD

Name ______________________

Address ______________________

DATE ______________________

CARD NO. ______________________

I am responsible for the books
I borrow. ______________________

DO YOU KNOW?

1. Where is the LIBRARY nearest your home? ______________________
2. How do you get there? ______________________
3. What is the LIBRARIAN'S name? ______________________
4. Do you go to your SCHOOL LIBRARY? ______________________
5. Should you let others use your LIBRARY CARD? ______________________

IX. Additional Topics

Daily experiences may become the basis for problem-solving adventures. One important objective of this book is to develop awareness of the wide range of problem encounters in the environment. Through a variety of topics, the range of possibilities is demonstrated, and a methodology of solution presented.

How can the teacher further expand upon the introductory ideas presented in this book? It is the teacher's responsibility to be alert to group or individual problems. For example, in one group there may be need for deeper consideration of self-concept problems, or another group may require intensive study of home, neighborhood, or community situations.

We begin with child-centered problems of self-sufficiency, bodily care, daily functions, the use of toilet articles and eating utensils.

The "Related Problems" section that accompanies each problem suggests other possible situations for further exploration. Each section is a fertile source for the introduction of new and related topics.

Example: Are you considerate when using other people's bathrooms? Why should each family member have his own personal toilet articles? Why should you brush your teeth?

Additional topics related to discovering oneself may include problems of physical growth and knowledge about the body.

Example: Senses — How do your eyes help you? How many sounds do you know? How do you know it is hot? Can you "smell" danger? (Example: smoke)

A large proportion of time is spent in the home. An adult must cope with problems involving the use of tools, machines and appliances. Therefore a retarded child needs pragmatic experiences which will enable him to function in the home. Furthermore, he may obtain employment in related areas as dishwasher, porter or busboy. At home and in such related environments, new gadgets (electric knife, can opener), machines (electric broom), appliances (steam iron, dishwasher), and packaging devices (spray cans) are in constant use. The topic dealing with dials and switches also offers many problem-solving possiblities.

Examples: how to "set" a radio, TV, refrigerator, clock timer, etc. The child should be made aware of measuring devices such as thermometers, meters and scales.

The teacher will discover many opportunities for demonstrating how to use new devices as they appear in the environment.

There are many phenomena or forces in our environment that affect our daily living. Examples: weather, season, time, water, electricity. The depth or degree of exploration depends upon the child's limitations. The goal should be, however, to stimulate the child's interest in his environment and to teach him how to cope with the physical world about him. The problem "How do different lights help you?" accomplishes this aim. Similar techniques may be applied to such topics as sound, air, or water.

Examples: water pollution, swimming, drinking water, fountains, etc.

Weather conditions and seasonal change are exciting, but they may present dangers for the child.

Examples: How do you use an umbrella? What happens when you get too much sun? Why is a slippery road dangerous? What kinds of clothes do you wear in the winter?

Living things are always of interest to the child. Plants and animals arouse excitement. There are simple, familiar experiments that explore the topic.

Examples: How do you care for plants and animals? Why do house plants wilt?

The physical world of the greater community also holds many constant and changing problems.

Examples: Where should you play? How do you use an elevator? Additional community topics may include use of public facilities, communication devices, and recreational facilities. Until recently, for example, the helicopter was not a part of our environmental scene. The heliport, airport, and marina are new places in our greater community. What are some other new places?

A topic is appropriate and timely if it helps the child improve his adjustment to his immediate surroundings. Similarly, knowledge of concepts such as color, shape, symbols and direction is meaningful. The teacher should plan further activities with these and similar concepts.

Examples: What are the colors and shapes of different foods? What other directional signs do you see at school, home, in the street? Other concepts may include size (big and little), weight (heavy and light), position (front and back), relation to space (under and over), time (early and late).

We teach the child how to use information and facts that will help him make a better adjustment to his environment. Our changing world is filled with directives, guides, coupons, applications and forms. The child wants to join the library or Scouts. He wishes to send for a FREE TRIAL OFFER of a new magazine. The filling out process (information) can present a problem to the child. It is a spiraling problem as he matures.

Examples: When he is ready for work he may need to answer an advertisement, write out an application form, and apply for health benefits. He must learn how to read directions on the label to prepare canned foods.

In the process, the teacher is not only increasing the child's knowledge but also discovering learning difficulties. As the result of a cultural or emotional limitation, information may not have been absorbed, or information may not have been provided. Therefore, a questionnaire such as "What do you know about yourself in an EMERGENCY?" becomes meaningful. The teacher is encouraged to construct similar questionnaires and develop other applied information problems growing out of the specific cultural needs of the individual child or of his social or ethnic group (see Chapter IV).

Example: What would you do if . . . ?

1. What would you do if you were alone in the house and a fire broke out?
2. What would you do if a strange dog came up to you in the street?
3. What would you do if the lights in your house suddenly went out?
4. What would you do if someone were sick and needed a doctor?

5. What would you do if you got on the wrong bus or train?
6. What would you do if you burned your hand?
7. What would you do if you were lost at the beach, zoo or other public place?
8. What would you do if an insect bit you?
9. What would you do if someone asked you to steal or take something that did not belong to you?
10. What would you do if you broke your bicycle?

There are many additional topics that lend themselves to the problem-solving situation. What possibilities arise from the following?

Examples: Would you do this? Which way would you go? What would you need? Which comes first? What would you say? How would you do it? Which one would you choose?

Whatever the topic, it should be one that stimulates interest. It may originate with an individual child, group or teacher. The important consideration is that it be meaningful enough to encourage children's participation through activities and thinking. Rote teaching methods stifle thinking. This is particularly true for the child with learning difficulties, who needs special teacher techniques to be motivated, stimulated and activated. The teacher uses provocative topics to accomplish this and to guide the lesson to defined outcomes and planned goals.

It is anticipated that the teacher will discover and explore those topics which will interest the child at his formative stages and have the long-range goal of preparing him for his everyday adult life.